TRUE BREW

A QUARTER CENTURY WITH THE MILWAUKEE BREWERS

by Chuck Carlson

Bob Snodgrass
Coordinating Consultant

Dan Hill
Commemorative Specialist

Jack Smith
Fine Books Specialist

Steve Cameron
Consulting Editor

Mario J. Ziino
Associate Editor

Larry Stoudt
Photo Editor

Anita Stumbo
Design and Typography

*Production Assistance by Kim Gates, Russ Reaver, Stacie Masterson,
   Bob Morris, Teresa Green, Jerry Steely, Michael Zahn*
Fiber Optic photo by Wolf Photography and Chris Dennis
Dust Jacket photo by Larry Stoudt
Dust Jacket Design by Bonnie Henson
*Contributing Photographers: Larry Stoudt, Ron Modra, Val Meyer,
   Chris Dennis, John Biever, Gary Weber, Al Frederickson,
   Dan Johnson, Jon R. Smith, Dale Guldan*
Select photos courtesy Milwaukee Journal *and* Milwaukee Sentinel
Remaining photos courtesy the Milwaukee Brewers

Published by Taylor Publishing Company, Dallas, Texas

ISBN: 0-87833-076-3 (General)
ISBN: 0-87833-077-1 (Limited)
ISBN: 0-87833-078-X (Collectors)

To my son, Brian . . . the future of baseball.

ABOUT THE AUTHOR

Chuck Carlson has spent the last four years covering the Milwaukee Brewers, Milwaukee Bucks, Green Bay Packers and the University of Wisconsin for the *Appleton* (Wis.) *Post-Crescent.* In his 15 years as a sportswriter, Carlson has also covered the Seattle Mariners, Seattle Seahawks, University of Illinois and Washington Redskins, though not necessarily at the same time. Carlson, a native of Bethesda, Md., is a graduate of the American University in Washington, D.C. where he received a B.A. degree in journalism. He lives in Appleton.

Contents

Acknowledgements   **11**

A Dedication . . . by Bud Selig   **15**

Foreword . . . by Bob Uecker   **21**

Introduction   **28**

1   **Balls, Bats and Bratwurst**   **72**

2   **The Braves Don't Live Here Anymore**   **86**

3   **Wallbangers and Other Wonders**   **104**

4   **Molly, Gumby and The Kid**   **132**

5   **A Cast of Characters**   **152**

6   **It's Been Fun**   **172**

7   **Deep, Deep Center**   **192**

Stats and Records   **206**

THANK YOU!!
BREW CREW
FOR 1982

BREWERS

Dear Mr Dalton's
"NO CHANGES"
WE LOVE YOU
JUST THE WAY WE ARE

Acknowledgements

LIFE'S PRETTY DARNED FUNNY, DON'T YOU think? Six months ago, any thoughts of writing a book, much less getting the silly thing published, was nothing more than a dream to me. A distant, unattainable, frustratingly abstract, dream.

But, well, life's funny. One little piece falls into place, wheels go into motion, things happen and — poof — you're an author. It really does happen that way sometimes.

Yet I've also learned that a project this immense can't be done solo. It requires so many people doing so many things in so many different ways. I always figured writing ackowledgements for a book would be the easiest part. But it's not. You want to say so many nice things; you want to thank everyone from your kindergarten teacher to the mailman; you want to make sure no one gets left out lest you be left off next year's Christmas card list.

But here goes anyway and, if I forget anyone, please understand — I'm new at this.

First and foremost, I have to thank my employer, the *Appleton Post-Crescent,* and specifically managing editor Bill Knutson and sports editor Larry Gallup. They showed incredible patience in letting me traipse around pulling this book together. They allowed me more than a little leeway and were far more accommodating than they probably had any right to be. I am most grateful. Thanks also to my co-worker Mike Woods, who did some desperately needed and much appreciated research.

In early July, when this project was still in its infancy, Steve Cameron all but told me I had no shot at finishing this by the assigned date. His stark pessimism was much appreciated and it spurred me on to do something I really didn't know I could do. I owe a lot to Steve. He called me to help him do some research on the book he was writing on the Green Bay Packers and he put in a good word for me when the idea for the Brewers book came up. He guided me through some rough waters on this project and he did a great job of editing the piece. It meant putting up with those miserable cruise missile-sized cigars of his, but it was worth it. Many thanks Steve.

As well, a huge thank you to Bob Snodgrass and Jack Smith of Taylor Publishing, who listened to Steve and took a chance on an unknown sportswriter. Thanks also to designer Anita Stumbo, who made sense out of this mountain of material and somehow turned it into a readable, handsome-looking book.

Of course, there would be no book without the cooperation of the Milwaukee Brewers, who bent over backwards to make this the best project it could be. Thanks to team president Bud Selig, vice president of communications Laurel Prieb, marketing vice president John Cordova, the crack media relations department of Tom "Sky" Skibosh, Jon Greenberg, Claudia Manno and team photographer Larry Stoudt.

Special kudos go to Brewers publications director Mario Ziino, who marshalled this project from the start and was a bigger help than he will ever know. Thanks a ton, Mario.

An enthusiastic and well-deserved pat on the back goes to Dennis Sell as well. Perhaps no one knows more about the history of the Milwaukee Brewers than Dennis and his insight, information and scrapbooks were invaluable. As well, thanks to Milwaukee Journal sportswriter Tom Flaherty, who helped fill in some huge gaps.

I'd also like to thank photographers Chris Dennis and Russ Reaver, who risked life and limb to get those stunning fireworks photos that appear in the front of the book. Thanks for the beer too, it didn't hurt.

Finally, a huge thank you to my wife, Theresa, who put up with a month of grunts, one-word answers and broken promises. ❖

A Dedication...
To all who are True Brew

AS SOMEONE WHO HAS LIVED AND DIED WITH every Milwaukee Brewers game since April 7, 1970, and dreamed about them for seven years before that, let me say that it has been a marvelous reality to call Milwaukee the home of the Brewers for a quarter of a century.

Vivid recollections run through one's mind when reflecting upon 25 years of history. Many, many good memories serve as a foundation to this franchise. But growth and development is enriched by failure and disappointment.

We all remember too well the early years when this franchise struggled through expansion and its aftermath.

Since the founding of this franchise our undivided purpose has been fixed on assembling the highest caliber team possible. There were times our aspirations fell short.

There were a great many other times we accomplished those goals.

We evolved into a contender in the late '70s with patience and hard work. The arrival of Sal Bando was a definite turning point. So was the addition of Cecil Cooper and later Larry Hisle. They gave this organization an identity.

Under the direction of Harry Dalton, and the guidance of George Bamberger and Harvey Kuenn, we understood what it meant to be a winner.

Since our American League Championship season in 1982, we have tasted success in many other forms. No club in the American League ever opened a season with a 13–0 streak as we did in 1987. Juan Nieves stands alone as the only pitcher in our history to experience the joys of pitching a no-hitter. Paul Molitor's 39-game hitting streak captured the hearts of a entire nation when he chased a dream — Joe DiMaggio. And who better to represent the maturation of an organization than Robin Yount, who became not only the 17th player in baseball to ever collect 3,000 hits, but one of only six to do so with just one team.

Those are memories for a lifetime. Those are keepsakes to build tomorrow's dreams on. They are unique to the Milwaukee Brewers. They are treasures for a generation to come. That is what makes this game special.

That is why this reflection on our first 25 years in Milwaukee was created. Not only is this a tribute to the players, coaches and managers who performed at County Stadium, but also it is dedicated to our fans. Your support through the years has been truly appreciated.

On behalf of the Milwaukee Brewers Baseball Club, I hope you enjoy this commemorative book, respectfully entitled: *TRUE BREW — A Quarter Century With The Milwaukee Brewers.*

Allan H. "Bud" Selig

*A Salute to the Past
and a
Commitment to the Future*

Sentry FOODS

Sentry Foods

Delzer Lithographic Co.

dlc DELZER LITHOGRAPH COMPANY

WTMJ

Miller Brewing Co.

Coca-Cola

Milwaukee Journal/Sentinel

Foreword

HISTORY HAS A UNIQUE WAY OF OPENING our eyes to life. Baseball has a special little corner in history books and now the Milwaukee Brewers have written their own chapter.

I can't begin to say how fortunate I am. My baseball career has certainly been a dream for me because not only have I had the privilege of playing professionally, but I also have gotten to broadcast this great game. I've also been truly fortunate because I've played and broadcast for my hometown, Milwaukee. That's more than anyone could ask for.

I've been in this game for 37 years, better than 23 as the Brewers play-by-play announcer, and it still amazes me that this organization is a quarter century old. I suppose my career as a broadcaster parallels the growth of this franchise.

I remember my humble beginnings. I had two of the greatest teachers in Merle Harmon and Tom Collins. They were the easiest and most helpful guys anyone trying to get into the business could ask for. Now, here I was an ex-player who knew the game. Well, it didn't matter. Up in the booth, it's a completely different story.

I got my baptism in New York. One day they decided between themselves, of course, to have me work alone. They left me in the booth. Now mind you, as long as I was able to play off of

them, I was fine. This time, they just left me alone. It was the fifth inning and I was there alone. I begged them to come back. I thought to myself, "What the hell am I going to do now?" I had no choice. I had to start talking. I talked about everything. I talked about what was happening on the field, in the stands and if I could see out in the parking lot, that too. It was good. They knew what they were doing. It was simply my time. When they returned to the booth, we had a good laugh. That was the start of it for me. After that, I had no problems.

After spending so many years here, I have seen what baseball means to this city. The events, the games themselves, sure they're important, but it's the memories that keep people coming back. And the Brewers have so many to share.

I remember when the Brewers played the California Angels in the inaugural opener in 1970. I remember Don Money's grand slam that wasn't. I'll never forget Cecil Cooper's game-winning single against the Angels in the final game of the American League Championship Series. And how could anyone forget the day Robin Yount's name appeared on the lineup card — twice.

Those tidbits don't even scratch the surface of Brewers history. Just stop and think for a moment and the memories will come flooding back to you too. Whether it was the early years with guys like Marty Pattin and Lew Krausse, and Tommy Harper and Danny Walton, the next generation with the Pedro Garcias and Bill Parsons and Darrell Porters or that awesome bunch from the late 1970s and early '80s, teams that may have had the best talent in baseball. Or maybe you remember "Team Streak" or Juan Nieves' no-hitter or the up and coming Brewers talent like Pat Listach or Cal Eldred. Yes, as long as there are fans, there will be memories.

I remember a game in County Stadium against the Oakland A's. Here were the world champs and they had the Brewers beaten. All of a sudden, the club rallies. No problem, in comes Rollie Fingers to shut the door. The place is going nuts. Here is the best reliever in baseball , pitching for the best club in baseball and the crowd is unnerving him and his teammates. Up steps an obscure player in Bobby Mitchell, who gets a big hit and beats Fingers and the A's. They weren't world beaters by any means, but they had their moments.

Henry Aaron gave this club credibility when he finished out his playing days back where it all began. He is the greatest home run hitter of all time and he gave a new generation of fans an opportunity to see him play. He gave American League fans an opportunity to see him play and that was a treat.

After the club paid its dues, it learned to win with players like Sal Bando, Cecil Cooper and Larry Hisle. Sal gave the Brewers an identity, Larry was known as a clutch hitter from his days in Minnesota and Coop, well he was

a steal. He was as pure a hitter as the game had seen in a long, long time.

Then there was that 1982 team, which I still think was the best in baseball that year. No rip on St. Louis, but I still think the Brewers were the better team. They were hurting down the stretch and I can only imagine what would have happened if we had a healthy Rollie Fingers, Gorman Thomas, Ben Oglivie and Pete Vuckovich. Are you kidding me? There's no doubt in my mind.

That club was so loose. They were constantly laughing and joking with each other and they were very close. But when the bell rang, they would go out together and beat the brains out of somebody.

My recollection is especially vivid of the final weeks of that 1982 season when the Brewers had to beat New York, Boston and Baltimore just to set up a showdown. That was the best division in baseball and any of those clubs could've easily won the pennant. Winning 90 games was common for each of those clubs.

In that final series against the Orioles, the Brewers needed one win to clinch the division. But the Orioles had beaten them three straight and kicked their butts doing it. That set up the finale and Baltimore had Jim Palmer, a future Hall of Famer, on the mound. I walked into that clubhouse before the game expecting silence and I saw just the opposite. They were loose and they knew they were going to win.

Then they go on to face the Angels, drop the first two games in Anaheim and then come back

to Milwaukee and sweep. It was amazing. Deep down, I think they had to do it that way to prove what kind of team they were.

And there have been so many other memories too. From Don Sutton's 3,000th strikeout to George Scott's taters to that talented trio of Robin Yount, Paul Molitor and Jim Gartner and so much more.

And where would this city be without Bud Selig? He busted his rear to get a franchise here. At the final hour, after years of blood, sweat and tears, his work paid off. I truly enjoy working for Bud. How many owners would allow someone like myself to take time off during the season to do all those Miller Lite commercials when the club was sponsored by Pabst? How many owners would give me the time off to go to Hollywood and do the "Mr. Belvedere" series? We go back a long

way. I've known Bud and his family for a long time. I don't look at Bud as only my boss . . . we are friends.

I'm thankful each and every day that I've had the privilege to be around this game. I love baseball and everything associated with it. It's not only what you see on the field that matters, it's the people that make this game great. I try never to forget them.

So enjoy this collection of memories because this commemorative book was prepared with you in mind. Hopefully, it will bring back many smiles and perhaps some tears too.

Bob Uecker

Introduction

ALLAN H. "BUD" SELIG STILL REMEMBERS THE day — that day — as if it were only yesterday.

He remembers the time of day, remembers what he was doing, where he was and, given a few minutes, he could probably recall the temperature, humidity and what he'd had for dinner.

No, there's very little about that day in 1970 Bud Selig doesn't remember, because it was the day all the sweat and struggle came to glorious fruition.

Milwaukee, his town, was big league again.

"It was March 31, 10:15 at night," said Selig, relishing the story for perhaps the three millionth time in his life. "Lloyd Larson, the *Milwaukee Sentinel* sports editor at the time, called to tell me. But I sort of knew already from my lawyers."

Sure he knew.

Deep down, he'd always known that some how, some way, Milwaukee would once again have a major league baseball team. And so it happened that on March 31, 1970, at — that's right — 10:15 p.m., Selig received official word from a federal bankruptcy court in Seattle that the floundering Seattle Pilots of the American League would be coming to Wisconsin.

Cecil Cooper labored 11 fruitful, though relatively quiet, seasons in Milwaukee. Even today, he is regarded by many as the best pure hitter in club history.

BACK ROW: Rob Picciolo, Ben Oglivie, Pete Vuckovich, Gorman Thomas, Randy Lerch, Rollie Fingers, Dwight Bernard, Robin Yount and Ned Yost.
THIRD ROW: Clubhouse Attendant Tony Migliaccio, Ted Simmons, Moose Haas, Paul Molitor, Don Money, Mike Caldwell, Mark Brouhard, Kerry Augustine & Jim Slaton.
SECOND ROW: Trainer John Adam, Visiting Clubhouse Manager Jim Kaicinski, Marshall Edwards, Roy Howell, Ed Romero, Bob McClure, Charlie Moore, Jamie Easterly, Vice President Tom Ferguson and Trainer Freddie Frederico.
FIRST ROW: Jim Gantner, Coaches Pat Dobson and Harry Warner, Manager Harvey Kuenn, Coaches Ron Hansen and Larry Haney and Cecil Cooper.
FRONT ROW: Bat Boys, Bob Virale, Bill Zinn, Steve Froemming, Jim Topitzes and John Booker.
Missing from Photo: Coach Cal McLish, Clubhouse Attendant Chris Sampson.

The long, bitter battle was over. For a paltry $10.5 million, Selig and his group of partners had brought baseball back to a city that still ached from the loss of their beloved Braves to Atlanta four years earlier.

The Milwaukee Brewers.

Selig would just roll the name off his tongue. The Milwaukee Brewers. Yep, it had a nice ring to it. And they belonged to Milwaukee. Even today, Selig shakes his head at the bizarre, almost surreal, way events transpired. The same man, rebuffed in his efforts to land a major league club through expansion, stunned when an apparent deal to buy the Chicago White Sox fell through, left behind in his efforts to buy the Pilots originally, had finally succeeded.

"It's an amazing story," he said.

Of course it is. What else would you expect?

And it's an amazing story that begins it's 25th season. Has it really been that long? Has so much time really gone by in what seems like the blink of an eye? Wasn't Robin Yount a fuzzy-cheeked pup of a shortstop just last Friday? It sure seems that

(Above) Nothing came easily to the 1982 Brewers, but for three straight Sundays in October, they kept Milwaukee and baseball on the edge of its seat with some stirring play.

(Opposite) One of the first great characters for the Milwaukee Brewers was George "The Boomer" Scott. He may have been a lot of things in his five years with the Brewers, but he was never dull.

(Above) Even from the back, there's no mistaking No. 44 — Henry Aaron — one of two players (the other is reliever Rollie Fingers) to have his number retired by the Brewers.

(Right) One of the great steals in the history of baseball trades was right-hander Pete Vuckovich. He was thrown into the deal that sent Rollie Fingers and Ted Simmons from St. Louis to Milwaukee in 1980, laying the foundation for a Brewers pennant in 1982.

way. Has it really been 11 seasons since that remarkable collection of characters won Milwaukee's first, and so far only, American League championship?

Has it been six years since Paul Molitor's 39-game hitting streak mesmerized an entire country? Six years since the Brewers fashioned a 13-game winning streak that included a no-hitter by a star-crossed flamethrower named Juan Nieves? And has Harvey Kuenn, still spoken of almost in reverence by his ex-players, really been dead five long years?

The time just slips away.

Those early years, admittedly, were shaky as they are with any new club seeking some identity. The Brewers also battled through some awkward teenage times as they desperately tried to find their niche.

But this franchise, through

good times and bad, learned some valuable lessons. Now the Milwaukee Brewers, born amid confusion and uncertainty, have grown up and developed into one of baseball's more consistent franchises. Though entering just their 25th season, the Brewers have posted one of the best records in baseball over the last 15 years.

"I think we've had a very proud history," Selig said. "For a team only 24 years old, I think we've built quite a tradition, which is unusual."

You know the names and the events that followed them. From those fledgling years with Tommy Harper and Danny Walton and Marty Pattin, to the developmental era with George "The Boomer" Scott and Jim Colborn. It continued into glory seasons when the Brewers featured perhaps the

(Above) B.J. Surhoff burst onto the scene in 1987 and remains a key element for the Brewers today.

(Left) Pete Ladd was another unheralded member of that 1982 bullpen, locking down the final game of the ALCS against the California Angels.

most fearsome collection of offensive talent this side of the Bronx and has continued to this day with Paul Molitor, Greg Vaughn, Cal Eldred and that 38-year-old man they still call "The Kid," the irrepressible Yount.

But what about some names you may not remember but were nonetheless part of the Brewers story, as well? Guys like Mark Brouhard, Bobby Pena, Bill Parsons, Ned Yost, Bobby Coluccio, Marshall Edwards, Dale Sveum and so many others. They're also part of the rich tapestry that has been the Milwaukee Brewers.

No, the Brewers don't have a World Series flag waving over venerable County Stadium — not yet — but memories could fill the old ballyard to the rim.

That's what this book is all about. It's a retrospective and a celebration of a team called the Brewers. It's about Chinese aviators and Rollie Fingers. It's about Hammerin' Hank and Bambi's Bombers and Harvey's Wallbangers. It's about Mr. Warmth

(Top) Wily veteran Don Sutton came up huge for the Brewers late in 1982. He went on to earn his 3,000th strikeout in his two-plus seasons there.

(Bottom) He had no managerial experience at all, but Phil Garner had the kind of experience you could only gain from playing in the big leagues.

and Lach's Legions of Doom and Vuke and Gumby. Heck, it's even about Bernie and Bonnie Brewer, "The True Blue Brew Crew" and "The Trade."

It's about where you were and what you were doing when California's Rod Carew hit that one-hop shot to Yount at short for the final out in the ALCS in 1982. It's about how the Angels crushed the new Brewers 12–0 in that first game back on April 7, 1970, and how you couldn't have cared less because baseball was back. It's about watching

Gorman Thomas stand at the plate daring a pitcher to throw some high heat.

It's about everything that makes Milwaukee a special baseball town and the Brewers a special baseball team.

Obviously, there's no way to squeeze 25 years worth of memories into one book. But we'll make a gallant effort, through words and a dugout full of photos, to take you back through a quarter-century of the Milwaukee Brewers.

For some, hopefully, this book will bring it all back. The smells, the sounds, the texture, the taste of that first bratwurst on opening day, the very essence that made a day watching baseball at County Stadium a day worth remembering.

For others, maybe it will jog a few special thoughts. Your first ballgame with your dad. The foul ball you wrestled away from six other kids. A special autograph from that one special player.

Obviously, this book will mean different things to different people. But whatever it brings back, here's hoping — first and foremost — it brings a smile to your face.

This is "True Brew," a look back and a peek ahead. Enjoy the journey and don't forget the sauerkraut.

— Chuck Carlson
July 1993

42

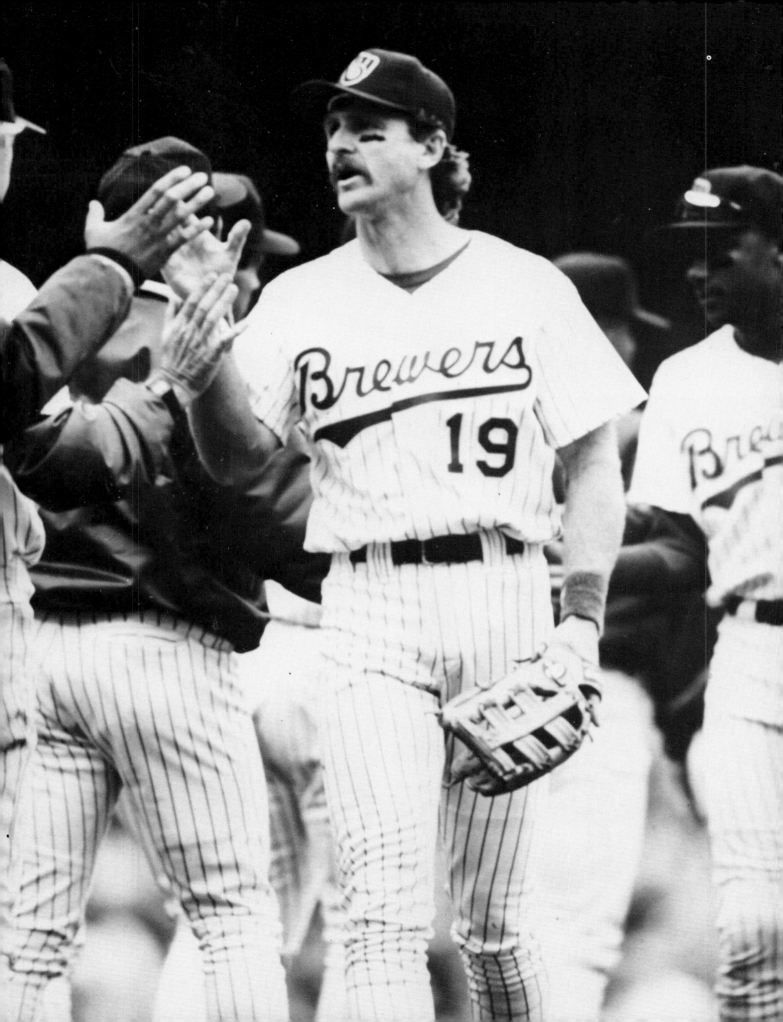

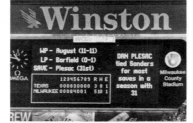

Chapter One

Balls, Bats and Bratwurst

STOP ME IF YOU'VE HEARD THIS ONE: YOU have to be sure to visit Wisconsin next summer, it's the nicest weekend you'll ever have.

Haw, haw.

Sure, there's this image about Wisconsin and its weather. And in most cases, it's a well deserved image. It can be downright nasty up here. But the hardy souls who live here only smile at the image. They know what it's really like. They know what it takes to survive. They know that, when planning to attend the Milwaukee Brewers home opener, it's probably not a bad idea to bring gloves. And a scarf. And maybe a blanket.

Just in case.

Yet that's one of things that makes baseball in Milwaukee so special. No domes here, no sir. Bring on the elements and provide the players who can handle them. It's baseball in its primal element and that's the way fans here like it. Contrary to popular belief, only two Brewers home openers have ever been snowed out and a season never has been postponed until June waiting for the drifts to melt.

And by the way, very few cases of frostbite have been reported. In fact, there are many visiting ballplayers who consider Milwaukee their favorite stop during the season.

"Milwaukee has always been my favorite," said Dan Quisenberry, the Kansas City Royals' former reliever who would think nothing of finding a vendor and scarfing down a couple of freshly grilled bratwursts before duty called.

It was always clear that Brewers fans didn't need much to support their team, just an understanding that their heroes were trying as hard as they could. And sometimes, looking back, it wasn't so obvious.

That realization was hitting some fans barely three months after the new team had come to town in 1970. Attendance was spotty which, not coincidentally, matched the play on the field. And by that point, Milt Mason had seen enough.

Empty seats, that is.

The 69-year-old retired aviation engineer couldn't believe that fans weren't flocking in droves to see the brand new team, no matter how mediocre it might be.

So on July 6, 1970, with a slight nudge from Brewers baseball operations director and friend Marvin Milkes, Milt Mason decided to take a stand.

Make that a seat.

And his publicity stunt would set in motion much more than he ever dreamed. This man, who would be known as the first and

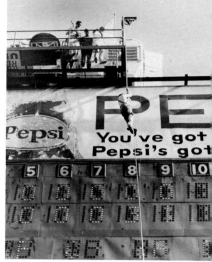

most influential "Bernie Brewer," clambered up 81 steps to the top of the scoreboard in right field where his vigil began.

In a specially constructed trailer that included a 21-inch color TV, a gas stove, an exercise bike, a refrigerator and two telephones (one to talk to fans and one to talk with the media), Mason took his place. His objective was simple: He vowed not to come down until the Brewers drew a sellout crowd.

When snow in August looked more likely, the stakes were lowered and Mason this time swore he would not descend from his cozy confines until a crowd of 40,000 showed up. In that time, Mason became something of a national celebrity and a local icon, leading many to wonder if fans were staying away on purpose just to see how long Mason would hold out.

Mason simply scoffed at such talk. "I'm kind of a loner anyway," he said.

One day, Brewers catcher Phil Roof showed up to scope out Bernie's digs. "Nice little place you got here," said Roof, more than a little breathless after the climb.

"Not bad," Mason said.

"Did they take the crane away that brought you up here?" asked Roof.

"Yup."

"They must figure you're going to stay a while," concluded Roof.

Did they ever.

Along the way, Mason learned some crucial lessons, like not to use binoculars while watching the Brewers batting so as not to enrage opposing managers who thought he might be stealing signs.

And then, finally, it was emancipation day for the big guy. It was August 16, Bat Day against the Cleveland Indians, and 44,387 fans squeezed into County Stadium and Mason — after 40 days in semi-isolation — descended

The legend of Bernie Brewer is born when, in July 1970, 69-year-old Milt Mason ascended a platform in center field and swore not to come down until the Brewers sold out a game. When that became unlikely, Mason settled for a crowd of 40,000. When more than 44,000 showed up August 16, Mason made his triumphant descent, sliding down a rope to the roar of the crowd, The Brewers, naturally, won the game against Cleveland.

After a few seasons, Bernie needed a companion, so Bonnie Brewer was born. One of them, Janine Feltz, gives a Baltimore coach a love tap.

Brewers manager George Bamberger, one of the more popular Brewers of all time.

from a rope so quickly that he suffered some nasty burns on his hands and legs.

"That was my idea," he said.

Of course, the crowd ate it up.

"It was a great experience but I wouldn't do it again," Bernie said. "I have no complaints. It's just that I don't like to do anything twice. I like to try new things."

And while Bernie knew that someday — that season — he'd get his freedom, even he admitted that his stay was "getting a little old."

Perhaps, but it provided what may have been the first real sign that fans in Milwaukee were ready to embrace their new, somewhat perplexing, team.

Naturally, Danny Walton, who was rapidly becoming a fan favorite, belted an eighth-inning double and reserve Gus Gil followed with an RBI single to give the Brewers the 4–3 win, thus making the day a complete success.

"That was the day Milwaukeeans took us to their hearts," said manager Dave Bristol.

Yes, Bernie Brewer was born that day. Ask any Brewers fan about Bernard. He is as much a part of Brewers lore as any player, as any game. Over the years, Bernie became perhaps the most recognizable mascot in baseball. His act, which evolved from the initial Milt Mason days, was always the same. Perched in the center-field bleachers in a chalet, he would slide into a massive beer mug every time a Brewers player hit a home run or any time Milwaukee won a game.

Not exactly the kind of stuff you'd see on PBS, but it was part of Milwaukee, part of the Brewers. OK, so maybe Bernie was accused by rival managers of stealing

signs, but, hey, it was only a game. Besides, no one could ever prove anything.

And Bernie, who became a regular in 1973, was discontinued after the 1984 season and then was brought back in '93, epito-

mized the kind of fun fans had at County Stadium. But more than a mascot was born that first year. The first stirrings of a love affair between the city and their team began to show, too.

"They are the best fans in baseball," said former manager George Bamberger, the lead assassin on a team dubbed Bambi's Bombers, in 1978. "You'd come into the airport there in Milwaukee and you'd be off to the side, but fans would always come up and

County Stadium has been the site of many wonderful events. One came May 1, 1991, when the Brewers and White Sox hooked up in the longest game in County Stadium history: 19 innings, six hours and five minutes. Willie Randolph, in the middle of this pile, finally won it for the Brewers, 10–9.

say 'You guys are doing a great job. Keep it up.' They were never rude or obnoxious. The friendliest, nicest fans you'd ever want to see."

Bamberger so enjoyed Brewers fans that he'd make a point to go out to the parking lot before games and mingle at the tailgate parties. After games, he'd head up to Ray Jackson's restaurant on Bluemound Road and join the patrons discussing that night's game.

And why not? The fans, the city and the Brewers share a bond that is almost mystical.

"They're blue-collar fans," said long-time second baseman Jim Gantner. "They like to tailgate and have a good time when they come to the stadium. But they

want you to play hard. When they're sitting in the stands, when they see you giving 100 percent, running out ground balls, diving for balls, they'll never boo you. They'll never boo you if you're giving 100 percent. They're always behind you as long as you're playing hard."

"It's a small-town atmosphere here compared to New York or Chicago," said Tom Skibosh, the Brewers director of media relations since 1976. "We don't have vicious fans. A Brewers player has to be really, really, really terrible for the fans to get on him."

And the fans have had their share of memories.

The only no-hitter thrown against the Brewers came in County

Summer Fashions For Sultry Days
The Balistrieri Boys Get Away With It
High Risk: How a Medical Chain Went Belly Up

Milwaukee
MAGAZINE

TREB!

Through raucous
winning streaks and
lonely losing slumps, the
Brewers' new manager
Tom Trebelhorn proves
all over again that it
really is how you play the
game that counts.

BREWER
BULLPEN
BRIGADE

Real Taste of Beer

MILWAUKEE SPELLS BELIEVE
C-O-L-L-OR
MILWAUKEE BREWERS

CATCH
FEVER
Brewers

HARVEY'S
WALLBANGERS

BONES
25

BREWER PIZZA

BAMBI'S
BACK !!!

Milwaukee
BREWERS

BERNIE
BREWER

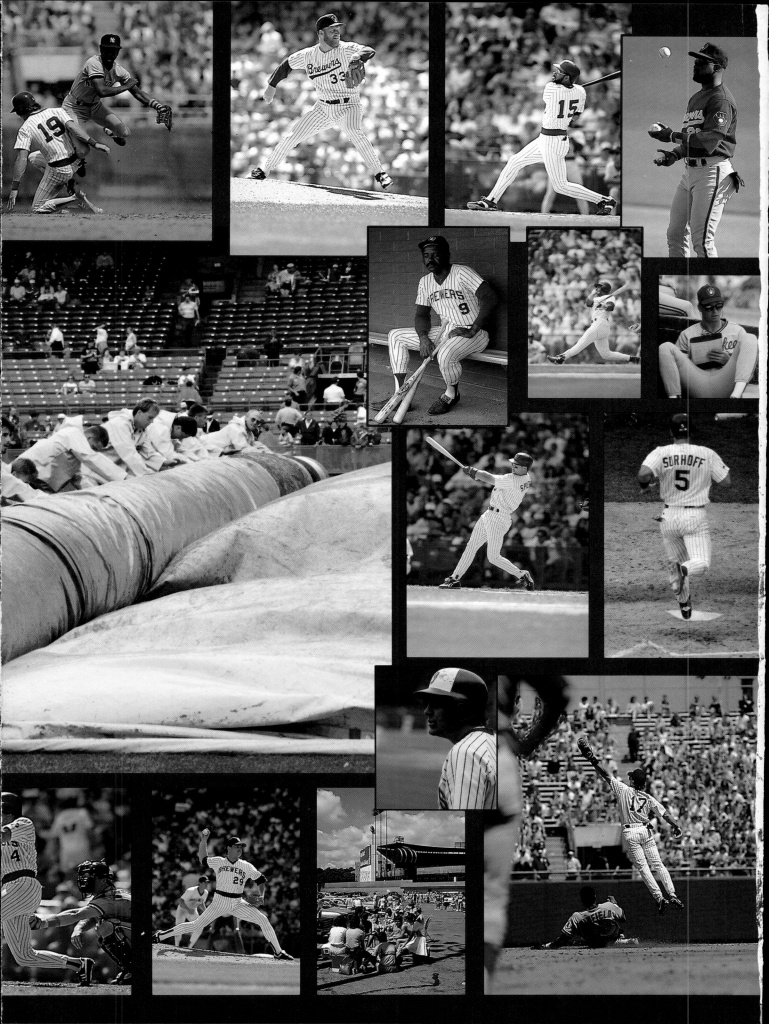

Come to Marlboro Country.

MILWAUKEE COUNTY STADIUM

milwaukee
brewers
BREWER FEVER

CIVIC WELCOME RALLY

Milwaukee Brewers

BREWER FEVER CATCH IT!
Congratulations Paul Molitor!

MILWAUKEE BREWERS

(Left) The end of an era: Bernie's barrel and chalet were dismantled in 1984 to make room for more bleachers. A fan vote, though, brought him back in 1993.

Stadium, when Kansas City's Steve Busby did the deed on June 14, 1974. Those were the dark days for the Brewers — the early, expansion years when the Brewers and the fans knew there was a light at the end of the tunnel but they just didn't know how many miles ahead it was.

There was Nolan Ryan, who won his 300th game on July 31, 1990, in front of 51,533 fans. That was a night that even surprised the venerable Ryan, who had seen almost everything in his 25 years in baseball. He was cheered the minute he stepped from the dugout to do his pregame warmups. Fans chanted: "Here we go, Nolan, here we go," like they were at some college football game or something. And Brewers manager Tom Trebelhorn could only watch in amazement and offer an explanation about why his loyal fans had suddenly turned, if only for a night.

"They want to see history being made," he said. "They're not necessarily rooting against us, but they do want to see history."

And they saw it.

They booed Texas manager Bobby Valentine unmercifully when he yanked Ryan in the eighth inning of a tight game. But Ryan got the win and he came out to acknowledge a crowd that really didn't need to do what it had done.

"It was real rewarding to see the Milwaukee fans react the way they did," Ryan said. "That really speaks well for them. It was a unique situation."

But unique is nothing unique to County Stadium.

It was the site where Paul Molitor's 39-game hitting streak ended in 1987 to a chorus of boos for the man who won the game for Milwaukee but cost Paulie potential baseball immortality. It was the site where frustrations ended in 1982 when

There aren't many more devoted fans than Brewers fans.

They probably have great jobs during the week.

Robin Yount threw out Rod Carew to give the Brewers their first American League pennant. It was the site where Yount made some history of his own, drilling his 3,000th hit in 1992 in front of 50,000 of his closest friends.

And so much more, too. There was September 14, 1991, when Detroit's Cecil Fielder hit the longest homer in the history of Brewers baseball, a gargantuan shot that cleared the left field bleachers and was measured at a staggering 502 feet. About two weeks before that, Brewers second baseman Jim Gantner hit a home run off Oakland's Dave Stewart, snapping a streak of 544 games (1,762 at-bats) without a dinger, the longest homerless streak in baseball at the time.

Remember that game on July 8, 1990, when the Brewers trailed California 7–0 in the fifth inning then systematically sent 18 hitters to plate on the way to a record-shattering 13-run inning? The Brewers went on to win 20–7.

Don Sutton collected his 3,000th strikeout at County Stadium on June 24, 1983, and Oakland's Jose Canseco stole his 40th base there on September 23, 1988, making him the first player in big league history to hit 40 homers and steal 40 bases in a season. Oakland's Rickey Handerson set a single-season stolen base record on the County Stadium turf too, swiping his 119th base on August 27, 1982, to shatter Lou Brock's mark.

Way back when, the Brewers Tommy Harper cracked his 30th home run on September 22, 1970, to become only the fifth player in history to steal 30 bases and hit 30 homers.

And, of course, there was Gus the Wonder Dog. Surely you remember Gus. He was hired by the Brewers to chase away a flock of seagulls — right, seagulls. Just when County Stadium figured it had seen it all, seagulls — hundreds of them — came off Lake Michigan and invaded the park during a series with the Yankees in June 1993.

It got so bad at times that play had to be halted while the birds were shooed away. Though the gulls had come to feast on moths who had set up shop in the outfield grass, many witnesses preferred to put an Alfred Hitchcock spin on it. And the phrase, "The Brewers play was for the birds," was quickly and mercifully worn out that night.

The birds were back the next night, prompting the Brewers to hire Gus to run them off between innings. Eventually, after several more days, the gulls went back from wherever they came.

It just goes to show, though, that just when you think you've seen it all, you probably haven't. Especially at County Stadium.

"People always say they remember where they were when President Kennedy was assassinated or when Neil Armstrong stepped on the moon," said Bob Uecker, a Milwaukee native, a one-time Brave and the Brewers radio announcer for years. "They also remember events in baseball like Bobby Thomson's home run, Willie Mays' great catch, etc. The same with Brewer fans."

This is Milwaukee. Girder and steel and concrete Milwaukee. Not glass and chrome Toronto. This is a city's city, unpretentious and not given to ceremony.

"Our fans are very special in Milwaukee because they are not afraid to laugh at themselves," said former manager Tom Trebelhorn. "They are not afraid to have a good time at the ballpark, and they are not afraid to just enjoy themselves."

When fans from other cities snidely referred to Brewers fans as "Cheeseheads," Brewers fans giddily took it as a compliment. Bolstered by outfielder Rick Manning, who wore a cheese wedge on his head in the dugout, fans rallied behind the phrase, calling themselves things like "The Curd Herd," and "Cheesehead or Dead."

"They turned around a derogatory term and turned it into a positive," Trebelhorn said. "That's just the way they are."

That ability to avoid taking life too seriously has proved a solid background for several Brewers. Robin Yount is in his 20th season

in Milwaukee. Jim Gantner played there 15 years, as did Paul Molitor. Charlie Moore played 14 seasons, Don Money and Gorman Thomas and Cecil Cooper were Brewers for 11 seasons and Jerry Augustine, who still lives in Milwaukee, played 10 years. So did Moose Haas.

Maybe it's no coincidence that so many players had long careers with the Brewers.

"I think playing in Milwaukee is the best thing that could've happened to me, personally, for my career," said Yount, who came to Milwaukee in 1973 as a soft-spoken 18-year-old shortstop with a superstar tag hung on him. He's been around ever since.

"The type of town this is is perfect for my style and I enjoy the small-town atmosphere over the hassles that go along with the big city. In that respect, being drafted and playing here for as long as I did is the best thing that ever could've happened to me,"

On a night strictly for the birds, seagulls invaded the County Stadium turf, searching for moths. It got so bad, the Brewers hired Gus the wonderdog to eventually chase them off.

In the County Stadium bleachers, on a sunny Wisconsin afternoon, there aren't many better places to be.

(Right) Pitcher Jerry Augustine takes a new prospect under his wing.

Yount said. "The fans have always been supportive. They've always been great to me and that's important."

There were others who seemed to epitomize Milwaukee and would've seemed out of place in another big-league uniform. Gorman Thomas, for example. No physical specimen, with a surly disposition and facial hair that wouldn't quit — could anyone imagine Gorman Thomas in a Los Angeles Dodgers uniform? Or with the Cincinnati Reds? Or even the New York Yankees?

Hardly.

"Gorman kind of typified Milwaukee," said Sal Bando, a former teammate and now the Brewers' general manager. "He sure liked his beer."

And Milwaukee loved Gorman. Through the good times and bad, he was their man, he was Milwaukee. When he was traded midway through the 1983 season, Milwaukee was shocked. But when he re-signed with the Brewers three years later, a meaningless three-game set with the Yankees drew nearly 100,000 fans, most of whom showed up to watch Gorman one more time. It seems there are just certain people who belong in Brewers garb, such as the bulk of that '82 title team.

With guys like Mike Caldwell and Pete Vuckovich — the '82 group was a true embodiment of the city and its attitude toward life. A blue-collar bunch, they had as much fun off the field as on.

"Baseball was fun in Milwaukee," Vuckovich said.

And no one really knew that until that 1982 season, when finally, Milwaukee was showcased on the national level. Through a tough five-game playoff series with the California Angels and a gripping seven-game World Series against the eventual champion St. Louis Cardinals, the Brewers showed America what baseball was like in the great white north.

"What Milwaukee has is a town and a team that were made for each other, blue collar and red-blooded, with sloppy moustaches and shaggy hairdos," gushed Art Spander of the *San Francisco Examiner*. "But they're not concerned as much about appearances as they are by results."

"Baseball is fun in Milwaukee," repeated the *Washington Post*'s Dave Kindred. "It's a war in Yankee Stadium, it's a beer jingle in St. Louis, it's a movie in Los Angeles — and it's a pep rally in Milwaukee."

Now, thanks to a fan election held in 1992, Bernie Brewer has returned and occupies the same spot he did in those glory days in the early 1980s.

"This is still a great baseball town," said current manager Phil Garner, who has built a club that relies more on speed and base hits rather than the titanic homers of the old days. "They know baseball and they have a lot of fun."

Some things never change. ❖

Chapter Two

The Braves Don't Live Here Anymore

IT WAS LIKE WATCHING FLOOD WATERS rising relentlessly toward the front porch of your family home — watching and knowing there was nothing, absolutely nothing, you could do about it.

Such was the feeling the city of Milwaukee had for its Braves. Everyone knew the Braves were leaving long before they finally did. It was a helpless, impotent feeling and Bud Selig felt it down to his soul.

A lifelong Milwaukeean, Selig had always dreamed as a boy that he would someday be the successor to his idol, Joe DiMaggio, as the centerfielder for the New York Yankees. But reality put an end to that.

"I was no Joe D.," Selig said.

Perhaps not, but he was something else. He was a fanatical baseball fan who would rather listen to Cubs and White Sox games on the radio than just about anything else in the world. So when the Boston Braves moved to Milwaukee in 1953, no one was happier than Bud Selig.

And for a time, it was heaven, pure heaven, as

Bud Selig was in his element in 1975 as he hosted baseball commissioner Bowie Kuhn and his city hosted the All-Star Game.

The Milwaukee Brewers, who just weeks earlier were the Seattle Pilots, get to know their new home.

The old scoreboard rarely had good news for that first team. It won only 65 games but drew more than 900,000 fans.

the city and its team melded into one. Behind stars like Hank Aaron, Warren Spahn and Eddie Mathews, the Braves went to the World Series in 1957 and '58, winning it all in 1957. And from 1954 to 1957, the Braves drew more than 2 million fans per year — almost an unheard of figure in those days. But soon, it all started to fall apart and Selig could feel it.

By 1963, the Braves had drawn only 700,000 fans and the rumors began. Still, they were rumors few in Milwaukee really paid much attention to until *The Sporting News* came out with a copyrighted story in the summer of 1964 that spoke of imminent disaster.

In 1962, the Braves were sold to a Chicago group that secretly harbored thoughts of moving the team to Atlanta. Selig tried to fight back, first buying up stock in the Braves and then forming a group made up of powerful local

business leaders whose sole purpose was to promote the team — and somehow keep it in Milwaukee.

But it wasn't working and Selig knew it.

On July 30, 1965, just months before the Braves officially left for Georgia, Selig formed Milwaukee Brewers Inc., in an effort to lure another major league team to replace the one that was about to leave. He'd decided to name the as-yet unknown team the Brewers in honor of the Triple A club that had played in Milwaukee for years.

"It had been a really good minor league team in Milwaukee for a long time," Selig said. "A lot of people went down to old Borchert Field to see them play. And after the heartbreak of the Braves, we really needed a pleasant name. It was a good name for Milwaukee."

Selig was backed by some of

Milwaukee's heaviest hitters in the business sector, including Robert Uihlein Jr., president of Schlitz Brewing Co; Robert Cannon, a circuit judge and legal adviser to the Major League Baseball Players Association; and Edmund Fitzgerald, chairman of Cutler-Hammer Inc.

But none of them mattered, not immediately.

After the 1965 season, the Braves left for a new life in Atlanta. Selig knew they would go, had expected it, and had figured he'd steeled himself to that eventuality.

But he hadn't. Not even close.

"No one will ever know the heartache, the frustration," Selig said. "After they left town, it was almost like a mission after a while. It was the idea that we'd been wronged, it wasn't right. It became my impossible dream."

That's exactly what it was. The odds against Milwaukee landing another major league franchise, especially after losing one so recently, were staggering.

Selig and his partners knew all that, but they went forward anyway. Selig himself went everywhere, anywhere, if he thought it would help his cause. He'd fly across the country to talk and listen and learn about what it would take to get baseball back in Milwaukee. He'd go to baseball's winter meetings and spring meetings, he'd go to the playoffs and he'd go the World Series — all in an effort to convince team owners that Milwaukee was worthy of a team.

"We'd look behind a potted palm, and there would be Buddy," Cleveland Indians president Buzzie Bavasi once said. At one meeting

in Florida, American League president Joe Cronin looked at Selig and said, "What are you doing here again?"

"I got to know the color of carpet in every major hotel in the country," Selig said. "But I grew up a lot during those times. The odds against us were enormous, absolutely enormous."

But that didn't stop Selig, who never quit believing in what was rapidly becoming his quest. Then came a ray of hope followed by crushing disappointment.

The National League was adding two teams in 1968 and Milwaukee appeared a good bet to get one of those franchises. At the announcement in Chicago, Los Angeles Dodgers owner Walter O'Malley proclaimed that San Diego would get one franchise and the second would go to. . . .

Selig recalls staring at O'Malley's lips as he formed the letter *M* — before he said: "Montreal."

And Selig left the room without a word to anyone. "I wandered the streets of Chicago all night," he said.

It got worse.

The following year, Selig thought — actually he knew — he'd struck an agreement with Chicago White Sox owner Arthur Allyn to buy that struggling franchise.

"We had a deal," said Selig, still incredulous even today.

At the last minute, though, Allyn's brother John decided to buy the team, once again leaving Milwaukee high and dry. Then, almost immediately after that setback, Selig received word that the Seattle Pilots, after only one season, were in fiscal trouble and might be available.

Perhaps no one was happier to be back in Milwaukee than pitcher Gene Brabender, a native of Black Earth, Wisconsin, who as a kid went to Braves games and dreamed of playing at County Stadium.

Some of the 933,000 fans who saw the Brewers that inaugural season.

But this time even Selig, the man who could find a silver lining in a mushroom cloud, wasn't going to get his hopes up because he knew what would happen if Milwaukee couldn't lure the Pilots.

"That was pretty close to it for us," he said. "If we'd failed there, I believed in my heart that was it. I don't think we could've kept the group together."

The state of Washington was battling furiously to keep the team in Seattle and filed a lawsuit to do just that. Then a Milwaukee attorney, Bud Zarwell, hit on an idea. Have the Pilot ownership, which wanted to sell to Selig, declare bankruptcy. The case would be heard in federal court and the judge would only be required to do what was best for the debtor and not force a local judge to be subjected to pressure.

When it became clear the Pilots couldn't pay their debts, baseball commissioner Bowie Kuhn, who wanted to keep the team in Seattle, reluctantly agreed to the bankruptcy plan. In April 1970, barely a week before the start of the regular season, Judge Sidney Volinn gave Pilot owners permission to sell to Selig and his group.

The five-year struggle was over.

"My favorite song was 'The Impossible Dream,'" said Selig, smiling. "Actually, it still is."

But what had Milwaukee gotten itself into? It had inherited a very bad baseball team and had almost no time to make arrangements.

On a snowy afternoon, soon after the news became official, Selig held a press conference in an effort to try and make some sense out of what had just transpired. He was asked, among

other things, what the Brewers planned to do about uniforms.

"Very simple," he said. "We just tear off the "Pilots" and substitute "Brewers" and we put an *M* on the cap in place of the *S*. Seattle's uniforms are fine, with some minor adjustments."

More adjustments would be needed for the new team, which had floundered in Seattle the year before. It was a gang of orphans, veteran players who couldn't latch on elsewhere alongside youngsters who had never gotten a chance anywhere else. Milwaukee knew nothing about its new team and the team knew nothing about Milwaukee.

"I'm sure we'll get a warm welcome," said manager Dave Bristol.

Uh, yes they did.

On April 5, the new Brewers flew north to open the season and were greeted by nearly 8,000 fans who had jammed into the Mitchell Field terminal to greet them.

"It's fantastic, overwhelming, incredible," Selig stammered.

At the downtown hotel where the players were booked in, another 200 fans waited. The sheer size of the welcome took even the players by surprise.

"I thought we would get a welcome," said outfielder Danny Walton, "but nothing like this."

Said catcher Jerry McNertney, who would be the subject of his own fan club: "I'm really overwhelmed by the enthusiasm of the people. I didn't expect anything like this."

Perhaps the happiest player was pitcher Gene Brabender, a native of Black Earth, Wisconsin. Brabender's uncle had taken him to a Braves game when he was 12,

(Above) Ted Kubiak always seemed to be involved in a late-inning Brewers rally that first season. His seven RBI against the Red Sox is still a club record.

(Left) Danny Walton hit the first homer in Brewers history.

and he'd made a prophecy. "I told my dad that someday I was going to play in County Stadium," Brabender said.

It was a blissful shotgun wedding featuring a city thankful for baseball and a team that, after virtual obscurity in Seattle, knew it was truly wanted.

"Sure it was an expansion team, but it had its characters," said Bob Uecker, long-time Brewers radio announcer, a former Milwaukee Brave and a native Milwaukeean. "They fit this city. They were blue collar. Milwaukee was hungry and fans here didn't expect any greatness. They respected and cheered the players who worked hard and they showed the fans that they really were trying. The fans liked that."

At last, on a glorious April 7, 37,237 fans made their way to County Stadium and reveled in 70-degree weather and baseball as the Brewers met the California Angels in the season opener. If anybody minded that the Angels strafed the Brewers 12–0, it didn't seem to show.

"Those fans were great," said Bristol. "They were just dying for something good to yell about, but we let them down. Maybe we tried too hard."

Lew Krausse went three innings, gave up four runs and three hits and was saddled with the loss. John Gelnar followed, giving up four more runs without getting anybody out, before George Lauzerique, Bob Meyer and John Morris finished up. The Brewers had four hits in that first game off Andy Messersmith, with Steve Hovley collecting three of them.

"Tomorrow? Well we'll show up," Bristol said.

They lost then, too, falling 6–1 to the Angels, and again the following day to the White Sox in Chicago, 5–4.

But history will record the Brewers winning their first game on April 11 when they scored four runs in the ninth to beat the White Sox, 8–4. Walton belted a pair of two-run homers and Rich Rollins, Russ Snyder and Hovley each knocked in runs in the ninth to win it. John O'Donoghue recorded the victory.

The first win in front of the hometown folks, though, took a little while longer.

Ken Sanders was the first quality Brewers reliever. He was named "Fireman of the Year" by the *Sporting News* in 1971 as he won seven games and saved 31 more, a club record that stood until 1989, when Dan Plesac saved 33.

The Brewers acquired Johnny Briggs from the Phillies in 1971, and he made it worth Milwaukee's while as he crashed a career-best 22 home runs.

In 1973, the Brewers drew a club-record 1,092,158, a staggering increase from 1972, when they barely drew 600,000.

Staggering through a nine-game losing streak, the Brewers finally gave a crowd of 5,320 on a 36-degree night what they'd been waiting for, beating the Boston Red Sox 4–3 on May 6, the first win at County Stadium in five games.

And five years.

Unheralded second baseman John Kennedy was one of the unlikely heroes, belting a three-run homer in the fourth inning to give Milwaukee a 3–0 lead. A light hitter, Kennedy only laughed when asked if he knew the ball was out of the yard.

"When I hit the ball, I just run," said Kennedy, who wore a brown felt cowboy hat with the words "Victory Hat" emblazoned on it. "I haven't hit enough of those in my life to really know what the feeling is like."

But while Kennedy put the Brewers in position to win, shortstop Ted Kubiak eventually clinched it with his eighth-inning solo homer. The Brewers also got a superb pitching performance from 31-year-old journeyman Bob Bolin, who went eight innings, allowing only five hits and striking out 10 — including seven in a row, which was only one off the American League record.

That late-inning rally would prove to be a trademark for the Brewers that season. They rallied 15 times in the late innings to win. In fact, the Brewers played an amazing 64 one-run games in 1970, winning 28.

And Kubiak, somehow, always seemed to be involved.

He won a game May 9 with a two-out single in the 10th that beat Washington, 3–2. The next day against the Senators, he hit a home run in the ninth to tie the game at 5–5 and then Wayne Comer's pinch-hit RBI single in the ninth won it for the Brewers. It was his only hit as a Brewer since, later that day, Comer was traded to the Senators.

In the second game of a doubleheader that day, McNertney delivered a two-out, ninth-inning RBI single as the Brewers won 7–6, swept the Senators and posted a giddy five-game winning streak, their longest to that point.

It was just the kind of season the Brewers and the fans dreamed of. They were competitive, fun to watch and appeared to feature some promising talent. Tommy Harper became only the fifth major leaguer to join the "30–30 Club" — hitting 31 homers and stealing 38 bases — and Kubiak drove in seven runs against the Red Sox in a July game, a Brewers record that still stands.

The Brewers finished 65–97, tied for fourth in the American League West with Kansas City. More important, they drew 933,690 in that inaugural season.

But what followed was a rollercoaster for both Brewers fans and the team. In 1971, Brewers pitchers threw a major league-high 23 shutouts and Ken Sanders saved 31 games, a club record that stood for almost 20 years. Unfortunately, the Brewers hit only .229 as a team (the worst in baseball) and, while winning four more games than the year before, they finished in the AL West basement. Attendance dipped to just over 731,000.

That was also the year Frank Lane replaced Marvin Milkes as director of baseball operations. Through the season, Lane lived

A familiar sight to Brewers fans was George Scott taking a massive cut at the plate.

up to his nickname, "Trader Frank," by making minor deals to shore up sore spots on the roster.

He picked up Bill Voss from the Angels, Johnny Briggs from the Phillies and Jose Cardenal from the Cardinals, all of whom contributed — especially Briggs, who crashed a career best 21 homers. But those deals were nothing compared to what Lane pulled off during the '71 World Series.

In the first blockbuster trade in Brewers history, Lane dealt Harper, Lew Krausse, Marty Pattin and minor leaguer Pat Skrable to Boston for George Scott, Jim Lonborg, Ken Brett, Billy Conigliaro, Joe Lahoud and Don Pavletich.

It was a start toward respectability. A very tentative start. But even that wasn't enough in 1972, perhaps the most frustrating year in Brewers history.

Because the Washington Senators had moved to Texas and into the AL West, the Brewers shifted to the East. But everything seemed to conspire against the Brewers in '72.

A player strike delayed the start of the season and Milwaukee was plagued by miserable weather all season. On the field, well, it was just strange all the way around.

For example, Conigliaro, a key part of that huge trade, simply walked out on the Brewers June 26

Del Crandall became the Brewers second manager in 1972, replacing Dave Bristol.

This is what many folks envision when they think of baseball in Milwaukee: A 13-inch snowfall delayed the start of the 1973 season for four days.

and fled for the seclusion of an island off Massachusetts.

He never returned.

The poor showing on the field also cost Bristol his job in May and Lane his own spot later that season. Bristol was replaced by Del Crandall, who didn't have much better luck.

Still, Scott knocked in 88 runs, Lonborg won 14 games and Briggs drove in a career-high 65 runs. But overall, the Brewers slumped badly, going 65–91 as

attendance continued to skid, dropping to 600,440.

For the first time, questions began to arise about the future of the Brewers in Milwaukee. It was talk Selig ended quickly.

"The thought hasn't even entered my mind," Selig said when asked if he considered selling the team. "All of us have great faith in Milwaukee and the Wisconsin markets. I don't think anything more has to be said about that."

But it was clear 1973 was a

It was a wild and wooly season that included a 10-game winning streak, that saw the Brewers a game from .500 as late as August 31, a 20-game winner for the first time and the phrase "Chinese aviator" introduced into the local vernacular.

Milwaukee Journal reporter Larry Whiteside asked Detroit Tigers manager Billy Martin in May if the Brewers could contend for the AL East title. Martin smirked and uttered the line Brewers fans still remember.

"If the Brewers can win with that club, I'm a Chinese aviator," Martin said.

No one really knew exactly what that meant, but it was a rallying cry nonetheless. On Detroit's next visit to Milwaukee, almost 42,000 fans were on hand for a double-header to tell Martin what they thought of him. And, of course, when the boos reached a crescendo, Martin was in his element and he bowed deeply to the crowd.

Martin also provided the perfect promotion as the Brewers held a "Chinese Aviator Look-Alike Contest" in August which drew more than 100 contestants and which was judged by Martin. It was the perfect remedy for a Tigers team in the midst of a pennant run.

"It was a good night with a lot of humor," Martin said. "It turned out in the manner in which it was intended — lots of fun. Around the country, people took it wrong and it got a lot of bad publicity. Here, it was fun."

Early that season, Martin appeared to know what he was talking about as the Brewers slogged to a 19–26 record through May 31. Then everything fell together.

Jim Colborn pitched for the Brewers from 1972-76 and was Milwaukee's first 20-game winner in 1973. He is still among the top 10 in just about every Brewers pitching category.

pivotal year for the Brewers. Another disastrous performance on the field and at the ticket office could've sent the franchise spinning on a downward spiral from which it might never have recovered.

Happily, that didn't happen.

Despite the home opener being delayed four days by a 13-inch snowstorm, the Brewers, according to Chicago White Sox GM Roland Hemond, finally made it "over the hump."

Two rookies that burst on the scene in 1973 were Darrell Porter (left photo) and Pedro Garcia. Porter hit 15 homers and Garcia finished second to Baltimore's Al Bumbry for AL rookie of the year.

The Brewers won five straight, got hammered 11–1 at Oakland, then proceeded to reel off 10 straight wins. After win No. 9, a 15–5 thumping of the White Sox in Chicago, the Brewers bused back to County Stadium and found a gathering of 6,000 die-hards waiting for them.

The following evening, despite tornado warnings in the area, a crowd of 22,796 saw Jim Colborn beat the Red Sox, 8–2, and put Milwaukee in first place. The highlight was when the small, but raucous, crowd so unnerved Boston reliever Dan Newhauser that he walked three straight hitters with the bases loaded to break open the game.

The streak ended the next night when Boston swept a double-header. And a shaky bullpen lost leads all season, including seven games alone against the Baltimore Orioles.

"All we needed was six or nine outs," moaned Johnny Briggs,

"and we'd have been right up there."

In the end, Milwaukee finished 74–88 — not bad, but far from what it could, or maybe even should, have been. Along the way, Colborn went 20–12 with a 3.18 earned run average, Scott hit .306 with 24 homers and 107 RBI and three rookies — catcher Darrell Porter (16 homers, 67 RBI), outfielder Bobby Coluccio (15 homers, 58 RBI) and second baseman Pedro Garcia (15 homers, 54 RBI) — appeared on the brink of stardom. Davey May also had a solid season, hitting .303 with 23 homers. He also chalked up a 24-game hitting streak, the longest in the American League that season and a Brewers record until 1987.

Even more encouraging was the fan support, which nearly doubled from '72, up to 1,092,158. And in the June free agent draft that year, new general manager Jim Baumer selected a promising shortstop from California.

Manager No. 3 in the Brewers brief history was Alex Grammas (left and above), a former coach for the "Big Red Machine" Cincinnati Reds. But he only lasted two seasons.

His name was Robin Yount.

As for 1974, it may be known as the year of the flop. Despite a club-best 76–86 record, disappointment reigned as no one played as expected. Colborn, May, Coluccio, Porter and Garcia all struggled. Losing nine of 11 in the middle of July started the descent and the Brewers never recovered.

Once again, the Brewers felt they needed a shot in the arm and on November 2, 1974, Milwaukee dipped into its past and traded May and pitcher Roger Alexander to Atlanta for an icon — Henry Aaron.

Sure, Aaron, an original Milwaukee Brave and by then the all-time home run champ, was in the winter of his career at age 41. But just the name Aaron was crucial to the Brewers. And the previous year in Atlanta, the season he broke Babe Ruth's home run record, he hit .269 with 20 homers and 69 RBI. So The Hammer still had some pop in that ancient bat.

"He gave us instant credibility," Selig said.

It was also a final chance for Aaron, who knew his days as a player were dwindling to a precious few, but relished the opportunity anyway.

"This is a good ballclub and the kids can do so many things," he said. "They're so gifted. All you have to do is get them to have faith in what they can do. They can win. They're on the right road."

Crandall, an old friend of Aaron's, was excited at the prospect of having him as a player and — even better — as a positive, veteran influence on a painfully young club.

"We'll admit he can't do everything he used to do as a complete ballplayer," Crandall said. "But he can still swing the bat. He's going to give us leadership by the mere fact he's on the team. He's a true superstar and he's still a player."

The Brewers themselves couldn't wait to play with Aaron, either.

Davey May, acquired from Baltimore in 1970, went on to lead the Brewers with 25 home runs in 1973 and was the top RBI guy in 1971 with 65.

37 degrees, but a crowd of 48,160 came nonetheless and the game was delayed 10 minutes to allow everybody to find a seat.

Aaron finally got his first hit in the third inning, an infield number to the hole at shortstop that scored Coluccio. The Brewers beat the Indians, 6–2, and Aaron shooed away reporters afterward, telling them to talk to Briggs, the guy who hit the critical homer to win it.

Still, Aaron admitted: "I felt like I was part of the game again."

It was apparent, though, that Aaron wasn't the same player he had been. He hit .234 with 12 home runs and the Brewers, though in first place as late as July 5, sputtered the rest of season, losing 59 of their final 84 games. Crandall was fired after that year and Aaron was offered the job — declining it out of his respect for his pal Crandall.

Instead, Aaron came back for the 1976 campaign and played for new manager Alex Grammas,

The many faces of Henry Aaron, who closed out his remarkable career with the Brewers in 1975 and 76. Though he wasn't the player he was in his early years in Milwaukee and later in Atlanta, he provided a vital steadying effect for a young team. In a salute to Aaron in 1976, even teammates asked for his autograph.

"How many guys get a chance to play with a guy like that?" asked Johnny Briggs. "The young people seeing him for the first time are just awed by the way he goes about everything, not boasting or drawing attention to himself."

In his first game with the Brewers, Aaron went 0 for 3 at Boston — fouling out, grounding to short and rolling out to the pitcher. He went 0 for 3 the next day, too, before April 11, which was "Welcome Home, Henry, Day" at County Stadium. It was the ex-third base coach from the Cincinnati Reds and their "Big Red Machine." Yet the Brewers faltered again, posting a dismal 66–95 record.

Perhaps the Brewers should have gotten an idea of what kind of forgettable season it would be after the second game of the season.

Don Money had apparently hit a game-winning grand slam off Dave Pagan to beat the Yankees, 10–9. But while County Stadium was going nuts, a familiar nemesis, Yankee manager Billy Martin, popped out of the dugout claiming first base umpire Jim McKean had called timeout before the pitch.

McKean, a rookie umpire working his very first series, sheepishly admitted that he had indeed called time but wasn't particularly forceful in making it known. The Brewers were pulled back from the clubhouse and Money was sent back to the plate, where he managed only a sacrifice fly.

"I hadn't hit a grand slam in the ninth inning to win a game in 10 years," Money said. "So I sure wasn't going to do it twice in 15 minutes."

The Brewers lost, 9–7 and a very long season had begun.

It was also Aaron's final year and it didn't end the way he'd hoped. Looking back, Aaron concluded that something had changed after that night in April 1974 when he broke Ruth's record.

"I think I lost a lot of concentration after that," he said. "The drive you have every day just seemed to disappear."

Aaron hit .240 that last year, with 10 home runs — his last, No. 755, coming on July 20. But

Tom Murphy was the bullpen ace in 1974, posting 20 saves and winning 10 games.

a leg injury hobbled Aaron for most of the final two months and he could only sit and watch as the Brewers stumbled. But there would be a final salute to the guy Mickey Mantle called the "most underrated player in baseball."

"Salute to Hank Aaron Night" was held September 17, long after the Brewers had fallen out of contention. Another 40,383 fans, along with Mantle, Ernie Banks, Vic Raschi (who served up Aaron's first homer), Eddie Mathews and others showed up to pay tribute to Aaron.

Even Brewers players brought

Soon after that frustrating season had ended, a change was under way.

Over the course of the next few years, the Brewers outbid the San Francisco Giants for free agent Sal Bando, Scott and Bernie Carbo went to Boston for Cecil Cooper, Jim Slaton was traded to Detroit for Ben Oglivie, Darrell Porter and Jim Colborn were sent to Kansas City, two minor leaguers were dealt to Cincinnati for pitcher Mike Caldwell, Larry Hisle was signed and a kid named Paul Molitor was drafted.

Then came the "Saturday Night Massacre" in November 1977 as Baumer and Grammas were fired, replaced by Harry Dalton as general manager and George Bamberger as manager.

"I knew during the course of 1977 that our talent was better than what we were showing," Selig said. "There were a lot of things I didn't like and the more I thought about it, I knew we needed to make sweeping changes."

And so it began.

After almost a decade of futility, the pieces were falling into place.

Finally. ❖

The Brewers new regime in 1978: Harry Dalton took over as general manager and his first act was to hire former Orioles pitching coach George Bamberger as manager. The rest was history.

(Right) Henry Aaron hit only 22 home runs in his final two seasons in Milwaukee, but the trot was still a thing of beauty.

cameras and got Aaron's autograph to mark the occasion.

After a two-minute ovation, Aaron finally spoke, saying, "I hope my presence has helped teach some kids on this club what being in the majors is all about."

Aaron then went hitless in five at-bats and the Brewers lost to the Yankees, 5–3.

"He wasn't the same player he was," said Jim Gantner, who was a rookie infielder in Aaron's final season. "But it was still a thrill to play with him. He was my idol when I was a kid."

Chapter Three

Wallbangers and Other Wonders

SLOWLY, ALMOST IMPERCEPTIBLY, THE TRANSformation began.

One piece here, another there and the jigsaw puzzle that was the new Milwaukee Brewers began to take shape.

From the depths of mediocrity in 1977, the Brewers suddenly moved into the upper reaches of baseball for the next six years, culminating with their first World Series in 1982. The transformation was amazing, almost unprecedented.

In some ways, it seemed as though the Milwaukee Brewers evolved overnight. But it wasn't that simple. It never is. What happened is that the Brewers front office made a conscious, concerted effort to improve the team in several areas. And they got lucky, which never hurts.

But prior to the time Robin Yount threw out Rod Carew on a ground ball in October 1982, to clinch the American League pennant for the Brewers, a lot of water went over the dam.

Go back to 1978. No one could quite put their finger on what had changed, but the attitude was different, clearly different. And it was surprisingly

Acquiring Cecil Cooper from the Boston Red Sox in 1977 was another major move in the construction of a championship team.

Sal Bando was the first big-time free agent signed by the Brewers. Though the ex-Oakland Athletic was also being pursued by the San Francisco Giants in 1977, Bud Selig and baseball operation director Dee Fondy literally camped out on Bando's doorstep to convince him Milwaukee was the best place for him.

The wait ended on that magical night, October 10, 1982. The Brewers beat the California Angels 4–3 to win their first American League pennant and County Stadium erupted.

optimistic for a franchise that had done next to nothing in its first nine seasons.

Still, there it was. A new manager in George Bamberger, a new general manager in Harry Dalton, a new team logo and new uniforms helped. But it was the new talent on the field that was really making the difference.

Guys like Gorman Thomas and Mike Caldwell and Cecil Cooper and Larry Hisle, guys who knew how to win or would die trying to discover a way to win — they got things rolling.

These Brewers offered a tantalizing glimpse of what the next six seasons might bring when Thomas, Cooper and rejuvenated outfielder Sixto Lezcano, who had bristled under the control of Crandall and Grammas, all belted grand slams in the first three games of the '78 season — an American League record.

A realization hit, really hit, early in July against the powerful New York Yankees as the Brewers pounded previously unbeaten Ron Guidry 12–3 and the next night

Larry Hisle drilled a two-out eighth inning homer off Goose Gossage for another dramatic win.

That's when Bud Selig became a true believer.

"I was driving home on a Saturday night after Hisle had just beaten the Yankees and I'm thinking to myself: "Goodness, gracious, after all the dreams and hopes, we're good. We're really good," Selig said.

"We could all feel it," shortstop Robin Yount said. "We knew we were getting better. It was like a gradual building process. We knew the pieces were fitting into place."

Not only were the pieces finding their way into the right spots, they were forming a fairly impressive picture — one that would take baseball by storm for most of the next few seasons.

"I knew it would happen, I really knew it," said Bamberger, whose troops became known as Bambi's Bombers. "That's the most awesome offensive baseball team I was ever involved with. Just incredible."

(Above) Veteran Larry Hisle was Milwaukee's first legitimate MVP candidate. In 1978, Hisle hit 34 homers and knocked in 115 runs and was runner-up in the MVP voting.

(Left) Mike Caldwell's sputtering pitching career was revived when he came to Milwaukee. In 1978, he won 22 games and was named the American League comeback player of the year.

Who's this guy anyway? It was a young, clean-shaven and not-quite-imposing Gorman Thomas in 1973.

Want to know where it all started? Where the Brewers finally said they'd had enough? That losing had, once and for all, become intolerable?

Try the winter of 1976, long before a 67–95 season season cost Grammas his job. Long before Bambi's Bombers and Harvey's Wallbangers. Long before any of it.

Sal Bando, the steady, classy third baseman who'd been a rock for the Oakland A's dynasty of the early '70s, declared free agency, anxious to see what the market would bear.

Selig and Dee Fondy, Milwaukee's baseball operations director at the time, saw their chance. They made a pitch, a hard one, for Bando — a five-year, $1.5 million deal, a king's ransom those days.

"We really wanted him," said Selig. "I was sick of losing and I knew Sal would give us instant credibility."

There was a problem, however. The San Francisco Giants, who were 2,000 miles closer and also in need of some credibility, were making a serious run at Bando, too.

But remember, Selig was sick of losing. Really, really sick of losing.

"I flew out from Milwaukee and Dee Fondy flew up from Los Angeles," Selig said. "We sat on (Bando's) doorstep until he agreed to sign with us."

Bando remembers it well.

"The big selling point for me was Bud Selig and the type of person he was and the way he came off," Bando said. "The sincere concern of having me come as a person more than just a player. I remember the Brewers wanted me from

Bando and Harvey Kuenn were two huge reasons why the Brewers began to take off in the late 1970s and early 1980s.

Called by manager George Bamberger "the best right fielder in baseball," Sixto Lezcano hit 28 homers in 1979 and was named the team's most valuable player.

the start. San Francisco came in late, but Milwaukee was always there. I knew they wanted me."

And the Brewers got him.

True, 1977 was another horrendous season, but Bando was helping a young team jell.

"I always knew winning was important," Bando said, "and then when I left Oakland and came here and we didn't win that much the first year, you realize how much you miss it. We were so used to it in Oakland and I think that's why they brought me here. They wanted a winning atmosphere. Then we started to get people who knew what it took to win."

By the end of 1978, everything started to take shape. The Brewers took the baseball world by force, finishing 93–69, a 26-game improvement over the previous season. They had the fourth-best record in baseball and led the American League in home runs (173) and six other offensive categories. On the mound, Moose Haas set a club record, striking out 14 Yankees on April 12.

Postseason accolades also poured in: Selig was named ex-

ecutive of the year, Dalton was general manager of the year and Bamberger manager of the year. Second baseman Don Money was the first Brewers voted to start an All-Star game; Paul Molitor was named rookie of the year by Baseball Digest; Robin Yount, Larry Hisle and Molitor were all selected on postseason all-star teams and Mike Caldwell, who went 22–9, was named comeback player of the year. The Yankees could verify that as Caldwell went 6–0 against the Bronx Bombers that year.

"You could see it coming together," Bando said.

It was also the first year Milwaukee had its first legitimate MVP candidate. Hisle hit 34 homers, drove in 115 runs and scored 96 more. He finished third in the MVP voting.

"And anytime we needed to beat the Yankees," said Dalton, "it always seemed Larry was at bat."

The following season, as the Brewers went 95–66, the assault continued. The Brewers tied or broke 73 club records, setting 18 season marks and five game records. They were second in the American League in home runs (185), doubles (291), slugging percentage (.448) and total bases (2,480) — all club records. They also finished among the top five in the AL in nine offensive categories.

Individually, the statistics were just as staggering.

Thomas, originally drafted as a shortstop by the old Seattle Pilots, had become a reckless, acrobatic centerfielder and a fearsome presence at the plate. He led the American League with 45 homers, drove in 123 runs, walked 98 times and struck out 175 times. He set 11 club records and in a memorable August, became the first Brewers player to hit 12 home runs in a month.

Thomas was one of Bambi's personal favorites, a guy who would do whatever it took to get the job done.

"I knew this guy would run through fences," Bamberger said. "I knew he'd hit 35 to 40 homers in the minors and I was convinced he could hit 20 in the big leagues. So I told him that. I said you can hit 20 homers and hit .250 up here. He said, 'I'll hit 20 homers and hit .260.'"

OK, so he only hit .244 that season. Bamberger didn't complain.

There were others that season who took a hammer to the Brewers record books. Cecil Cooper, considered by most longtime Brewers watchers as the best pure hitter Milwaukee has ever had, hit .308, tied for the league lead with 44 doubles and carved out a 16-game hitting streak. He added 24 home runs and 106 RBI.

Left fielder Ben Oglivie, who joined Cooper by hitting three

home runs in a game, hit .282, pounded out 28 homers and 81 runs batted in.

Want more?

Molitor, who had moved to second base that season, was second in the AL with a club-record 16 triples and hit .322 (another club record) while Lezcano — whom Bamberger called "the best right fielder in the American League and maybe in baseball" — had a .573 slugging percentage, a .321 average, 28 home runs and in one stretch, hit four homers in four games.

On the mound, the Brewers threw a major league-best 61 complete games and gave up only 381 walks, the lowest in baseball. Caldwell and young hotshot Lary Sorensen each won 16 games and Jim Slaton, reacquired from Detroit the previous off-season, won a career-best 15 games.

There was also a run in May when Brewers pitchers threw seven straight complete games — two apiece by Sorensen and Slaton, one each from Moose Haas, Bill Travers and Caldwell.

But with all those massive

Don Money, who always seemed to get lost in the shuffle, was as steady an infielder as there was in baseball.

Though his career was cut short in 1979 by an injury, Larry Hisle always seemed to come up with the big hit when needed — especially against the hated New York Yankees.

111

(Above) A kid from Minnesota named Paul Molitor barely stopped in the minor leagues before surging into the Brewers lineup in 1978.

(Right) Two old-timers who meant a lot to the Brewers — Sal Bando and Larry Hisle.

numbers, only one really counted: eight. That was the number of games the Brewers finished behind the polished and powerful Baltimore Orioles. The Brewers had made huge strides, but they also realized how far they still had to go.

It seemed 1980 might be the year Milwaukee would put it all together, especially with such a competitive season under its belt. But problems began early and never really subsided.

On March 6, Bamberger suffered a mild heart attack and third base coach Buck Rodgers was named acting manager March 10 when Bamberger needed surgery.

Rodgers was able to keep the Brewers together when a players strike was called April 1 and extended through the end of spring training.

"We had a meeting with the players at the time of the strike and I told them if they were going to stick around, then it would be a total effort," Rodgers said. "They would show up on time and every day, not just when they felt like it. We had tremendous cooperation from (player representative) Buck

Martinez and the team and that left me with a good feeling going into the season."

That feeling lingered a while as the Brewers posted a 26–21 record and were only 5½ games out of first place when Bamberger, rejuvenated after heart surgery, returned June 6.

"The doctors said I didn't need the surgery but I had it anyway," Bamberger said. "And two months to the day that I had the surgery, I was back managing. But that was probably the biggest mistake I made. I shouldn't have come back that year."

With good reason. No sooner had Bambi returned then Paul Molitor, who was leading the league with a .358 batting average, tore a rib cage muscle and that caused him to miss the next 38 games.

Still, the Brewers were 43–34 at the All-Star break, 7½ games behind the Yankees. But despite a remarkable season from Cecil Cooper — he led the league in RBI with 122 (a team record) and was second in batting average at .352 — the Brewers came up short again. On top of that, Bamberger decided on September 5 to retire, officially handing the job over to Rodgers.

"I figured if I didn't reach my goal (of managing in the big leagues) by a certain time, then I would get out of the business," Rodgers said. "It's nice to know I reached it with a couple of years to spare."

The 1980 Brewers set 65 more club records and led the American League in four offensive categories (homers, RBI, slugging percentage and total bases). They also hit a club-record seven homers in one game against Cleveland. Still, they couldn't get over the hump, finishing 86–76.

Once again, however, more pieces fell into place for the Brewers as they continued their quest toward the top of the American League.

At the winter baseball meetings in Dallas that December, the Brewers made their next, and probably biggest, move. The Brewers had everything they needed to be a champion — except for a closer, a overpowering reliever who could come in and slam the door on late-inning rallies.

Down in Dallas, the wheels were turning in GM Harry Dalton's head. He knew the St. Louis Cardinals had just acquired stopper extraordinaire Rollie Fingers from San Diego. He also knew that the Cardinals had just picked up another superb reliever in Bruce Sutter.

And nobody needed two.

As a result, Dalton went to the Cardinals with an intriguing proposal — the Brewers would give up two pitchers, rookie Dave LaPoint and veteran Lary

Sorensen, talented outfielder Sixto Lezcano and a minor league gem in David Green. In return, they wanted Finger and veteran catcher Ted Simmons. The Cardinals were interested and would throw in another pitcher, Pete Vuckovich, as well.

The deal was all but done except for one tiny problem — the Brewers minor league people didn't want to relinquish Green, a player they thought was on his way to becoming a big league superstar.

"There were shouting matches between the major league and minor league people," said Tom Skibosh, the Brewers director of media relations.

"No," agreed Dalton, "they didn't want to give Green up."

But the deal was finally struck and the Brewers not only added another power hitter, they obtained two eventual Cy Young Award winners.

"Suddenly there were three things we needed: a starter, a reliever and a catcher with a strong bat," Dalton said. "The deal was just too good for us not to make."

Today, it is still referred to by Brewers fans as "The Trade."

Dalton still rates that deal as one of the better trades of his long big-league career, and even that might be an understatement.

Fingers went on to enjoy perhaps the best year a reliever could have, and yet the 1981 strike-wracked season didn't start out on any particular high note.

In April, as the Brewers struggled to a 9–7 start, Fingers went 0–1, appeared in seven games and saved only one, though his earned run average was a microscopic 0.53.

Fingers and the Brewers finally caught fire when the strike hit,

He came off as brusk sometimes, but Gorman Thomas was really shy in public. He was also the team leader in handing out nicknames. And while he never looked the part, few centerfielders were more daring that Thomas.

The forearms on Ben Oglivie show just how much power he possessed. He's fourth all-time in Brewers history with 176 home runs.

ing a ridiculously low 0.72 ERA. He was involved in 12 of the last 15 wins, the final one coming October 3 when he fanned Detroit's Lou Whitaker to secure a 2–1 victory and the second-half AL East title.

For the season, Fingers went 6–3 with a 1.04 ERA and a league-high 28 saves. He won the Cy Young Award and was named the AL's most valuable player.

The other members of "The Trade" didn't do so badly, either, as Vuckovich went 14–4 and Simmons hit 14 homers and knocked in 61 runs.

But there it was, the Brewers were finally in the playoffs, bastardized system or not. Unfortunately for them, it appeared as though it would be a short stay as the Yankees roared out to a two-game lead with 5–3 and 3–0 wins — in Milwaukee. But the Brewers battled back in the Bronx.

Molitor and Simmons hit home runs and Fingers picked up the win as the Brewers survived 5–3. The next night, Vuckovich, sidelined earlier in the series with the flu, shook off a 103-degree temperature he'd had only three days before and outdueled New York's Rick Reuschel. Fingers got the save, the Brewers won 2–1 and the series was tied.

The final game in New York saw the Yankees get homers from Rick Cerone, Oscar Gamble and Reggie Jackson and they advanced, 7–3.

But everything that had happened — all the disappointment, all the uncertainty, all the questions — were a mere prelude to what was to come.

As with any team or individual who wins a championship, all the

wiping out 53 games and forcing a split season to determine a champion.

The Yankees were the AL East's first-half champs and would face the winner of the second half in a five-game playoff to determine who would play the AL West rep and, eventually, who would represent the American League in the World Series.

In the second half, the Brewers hopped on Fingers' back and held on. Milwaukee posted a 31–22 second-half mark and Fingers was involved in 21 of those victories, saving 16, winning five and post-

(Above) Jim Slaton had suffered with the Brewers through the early years and was back (after a year with the Detroit Tigers) to help lead them into the future.

(Left) General Manager Harry Dalton (middle) announces that George Bamberger (right) has resigned due to health problems and that Buck Rodgers (left) would take over in 1981.

Lary Sorensen threw a team-high 235 innings in 1979.

parts must come together in perfect synchronization. There has to be that right mix of talent and destiny, of perseverance and simple blind luck.

The 1982 Brewers got all of that.

"That year, it was all just perfect," Molitor said.

Well, maybe not quite perfect, but pretty close. This was a team that excelled by using equal parts of the Brewers distant past, more recent past and current stars. Players who had been around during the miserable early days — like Don Money, Jim Slaton and, of course, Robin Yount — were melding with newer stars like Vuckovich, Cooper and Don Sutton to create a championship team.

"Everyone felt that 1982 was going to be our year," said Vuckovich, who would seize the Cy Young Award that season with an 18–6 record. "It was a confident team. It was an experienced team, a veteran team. They knew baseball and they didn't make a lot of mental mistakes."

But despite all that talent and all those expectations, by June 2, the Brewers weren't bowling anybody over. They sat 23–24, seven games out of first place and going absolutely nowhere under the authoritarian hand of Buck Rodgers.

So it was time to pull the trigger.

Prior to the final game of a series in Seattle, Dalton fired Rodgers and installed hitting coach Harvey Kuenn, a native Milwaukeean and a player favorite, as manager.

"We were close to 50 games into the season and by that time the club wasn't responding the way it should," Dalton said. "I felt Buck didn't have a handle on it at the time. I thought he could manage, but I didn't think he was the man for that club at the time. I felt Harvey knew them all, they liked him and respected him. He lifted a blanket off the club."

"Harvey was the final piece in the puzzle," Yount said.

Dalton was in the Brewers clubhouse at the Kingdome when Kuenn addressed the players for the first time as manager.

"He said, 'I know you guys can play, I know what you can do, now just go out and have fun,'" Dalton said.

Rodgers never quite fit as manager even though he helped lead the Brewers to their first playoff appearance in 1981.

Bambi in a rare moment of relaxation.

So they did and the Brewers immediately responded to Kuenn's low-key, affable style.

"I wish I could tell you I was clairvoyant about that," Dalton said. "But I wasn't. I just knew the players would play for him and they did."

"Harvey was intense," said Yount. "Harvey wasn't easy-going when the game started. He was the nicest guy in the world, but when the game started he was out there to fight. When it came time to go between the lines, he was out there for war."

Kuenn never claimed to be a genius concerning strategy, but he knew chemistry and he knew what worked. He knew what his starting lineup was, he knew his designated hitters were Roy Howell and Don Money and he knew he'd have Ned Yost catch once a week to spell Simmons.

Simple. But effective.

"Harvey was a player's manager," Money said. "He let you go out and have fun and we weren't having fun early."

"He was perfect for us," said Gantner. "I remember I always came into the clubhouse and I never had to look at the lineup because you knew you were in there."

Dalton: "We had a lot of good offensive players, a lot of individuals. On other clubs, they might not have fit together as well as they did here."

In Kuenn's first game, Milwaukee won 5–2 behind Caldwell (who would go on to win 15 games the rest of the season). The ball was rolling. On June 6, after the Brewers completed a three-game sweep of Oakland in which they outscored the A's 28–6, Cecil Cooper came up with the perfect nickname for this bunch — Harvey's Wallbangers.

They won 20 of 27 games in June and 11 of their first 15 in July, moving into first place July 11 after an 8–5 win over Kansas City.

"We started to play so good that we came to the ballpark knowing we were going to win," said reserve infielder Ed Romero.

And they came to the ballpark to inflict as much damage on a pitcher's earned run average as possible, too.

Six Brewers drove in more than 70 runs that season and four —

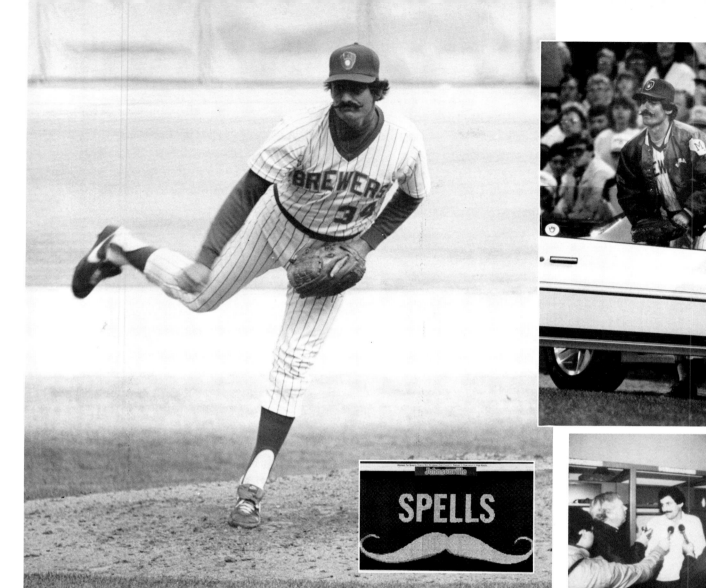

Thomas, Oglivie, Cooper and Yount — knocked in more than 100. The Brewers also crashed 216 home runs, the most in baseball since 1964, they hit 35 homers in one 15-game stretch, and they finished with a staggering team batting average of .279.

The Bangers hit back-to-back homers 16 times that season, tying the major league record set by the 1977 Boston Red Sox, and they hit three in a row three times. They also led the majors in runs scored (891), RBI (843), total bases (2,606) and slugging percentage (.464).

"It was contagious," said Yount. "You saw all these big hitters and you find you're doing it, too."

And Yount should know. Already a nine-year veteran in the big leagues, Yount had established himself as a solid, but relatively unspectacular, player. Always known as a superb defensive shortstop, his offensive production had never caused that much of a stir.

It did in '82.

That season, Yount erupted onto the baseball scene, finishing among the league leaders in seven categories. He hit .331,

Rollie Fingers virtually carried the Brewers to their second-half division title in the strike-shortened 1981 seasons. In fact, his 1.04 ERA and 29 saves insured Fingers a Cy Young Award.

(Above) Pete Vuckovich won a total of 32 games in 1981 and 1982, earning a Cy Young Award for his 18-6 campaign in '82.

"The Trade" brought Vuckovich, catcher Ted Simmons and Rollie Fingers to Milwaukee. They were the final pieces in the Brewers championship puzzle.

(Right) Mike Caldwell especially flourished under Kuenn's light hand. He struggled early in 1982, but after Kuenn took over, he won 15 games.

winding up second in the American League by a single point to Kansas City's Willie Wilson. He led the AL in hits (210) and total bases (367), tied Kansas City's Hal McRae for most doubles with 46, was second in runs (129), was third in triples (12) and fourth in RBI with 114. Oh, and by the way, he also hit 29 homers, stole 14 bases and won a Gold Glove for his extraordinary play at short. From August on, Brewers fans seemed to know what was coming, for every time Yount came to the plate, they'd chant "MVP, MVP. . . ."

"He's the best all-around shortstop I've ever seen play," Kuenn said.

Yount also was named the American League MVP, the second straight season a Brewers player had won that award and the first time a team had swept MVP and Cy Young honors in back to back years.

But while Yount was having an unconscious season and while the Brewers were rocketing baseballs into orbit, the Orioles were still hanging around like gum on the bottom of a shoe.

And concern began to grow when, in early September, Fingers, who'd rung up 29 more saves, was lost for the season with an arm injury. At the same time, the Brewers made a deal with Houston to acquire the wily veteran Sutton. As it turned out, they needed him, despite the fact they held a six-game lead heading into September.

Still, the Brewers appeared in excellent shape as they headed into Boston for the next to last series of the regular season.

In a year of dramatic victories,

perhaps the most dramatic came in that series, and it was tinged with more than a little irony.

Ned Yost, the seldom used catcher who didn't even pack his bats for the trip to Boston, came on in the eighth inning of a 3-3 game to replace Simmons, who had left for a pinch-runner. In the ninth, Yost came up with Molitor on second and Cooper, who was intentionally walked, on first. The opponent was Mark Clear, one of the top relievers in the league that season, and Yost was using a bat borrowed from Charlie Moore.

Yost had never faced Clear before but, he conceded, "There are a lot of pitchers I've never faced."

In this storybook season, what else could happen but a storybook finish? On a 1-0 pitch, Yost drilled a Clear fastball into the netting atop Fenway Park's Green Monster in left for a three-run, game-winning homer — his only dinger of the season.

The Brewers, usually a workmanlike and unemotional group, erupted in the dugout.

"I never had any idea, really," a flabbergasted Yost said afterward. "I saw it going up. I didn't have any idea it might go out until I saw Jim Rice playing the wall. I thought, 'Hey, that's got as chance of hitting the wall.' Then it went into the net. I couldn't believe it. I was overjoyed. I wanted to jump up and down, but I didn't think that was the thing to do. So I just ran around the bases."

"The way it turned out, it was a stroke of genius," Kuenn said. "Not on my part — it was a stroke of genius on Ned Yost's part."

That win, coupled with a Baltimore loss that night, put the

The players called him "Archie," but no one garnered more respect than Harvey Kuenn. He took over a floundering team early in 1982 and turned them into pennant winners.

He had been a solid offensive player for years, but in 1982, Robin Yount erupted on the scene, hitting .331, with 29 homers and 114 RBI. He won a Gold Glove at shortstop and was named the league MVP.

Brewers up by four games with five to play. The math was easy to do.

The next night, Boston beat the Brewers 9–4 and Baltimore won, too, giving the Brewers a three-game lead with four to play.

"Now they have to beat the team they're in it with," said Boston reliever Bob Stanley. "That's the way it should be."

Was it ever.

In a remarkable four-game series that took Brewers fans from the depths of despair to the very heights of euphoria, the Brewers and Orioles whacked away at each other at Baltimore's Memorial Stadium.

The Orioles, in fact, were playing better baseball at the end of the season than Milwaukee, winning 33 of their last 43, including 17 come-from-behind victories. It continued on a Friday night when the Orioles swept a doubleheader, 8–3 and 7–1, beating both Vuckovich and Caldwell and shaving the Brewers' lead to one game.

It continued the next day when the Orioles crushed the Brewers 11–3. That set up one more

game, for all the marbles, on Sunday, October 3.

"This team's whole season comes down to one game, which is not the way we had it planned," said Doc Medich, the losing pitcher on Saturday.

Still, Sunday's finale offered a delicious matchup between the veteran, established Orioles and the young upstarts who wanted to knock them off their perch. It also offered a pitching matchup of Sutton, who'd won 257 career games, and Jim Palmer, winner of 263.

"I guess we're going to see what kind of character this team's got," said Jim Gantner.

Mario Ziino, the Brewers publications director, remembers a remarkable car ride with GM Harry Dalton from the team hotel to Memorial Stadium prior to the showdown.

Dalton was so confident, so sure of his team that even an uncertain Ziino was becoming a believer.

"By the time we got to the park, I was convinced we were going to win too," he said.

Dalton closed the clubhouse door and every Brewers player turned his eyes toward him.

"I'm disappointed we lost but I'm not disappointed in you," Dalton told them.

Dalton talked to each player individually, exhorting him to keep up the good work, to never give up.

"It was the most inspiring talk I'd ever heard," Ziino said.

Dalton finally laughed and said, "Let's win this thing."

On the final day of the season, in front of 52,000 hostile fans, in what was supposed to be the last

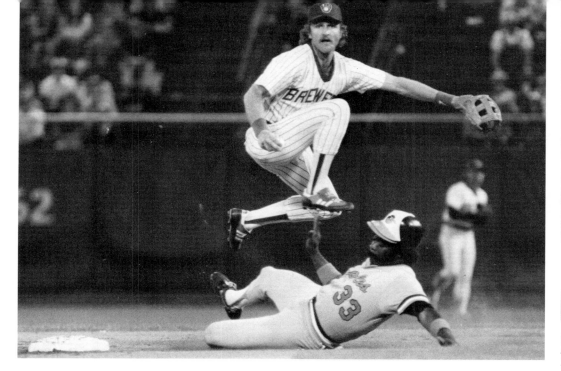

(Above) The Brewers traded for Don Sutton in late August 1982 and he would prove to be a huge acquisition, winning that epic showdown with the Orioles on the final day of the regular season.

(Left) Robin Yount performs his special acrobatics at shortstop.

Cecil Cooper pounded out 205 hits in 1982, joining Yount and Paul Molitor in the 200-hit club that season.

game for Oriole manager Earl Weaver, the Brewers proved themselves.

"You had two great pitchers going at it," Ben Oglivie said. "What are the percentages of two teams playing the final game like that for the championship? That's what it's all about. You couldn't have had a better four-game series."

"It was a very positive attitude in the clubhouse before the game," Gantner said. "We just knew we were going to win. We had come too far to lose it now."

"Memorial Stadium was rocking," radio announcer Bob Uecker recalled. "The crowd was deafening and these guys are in the clubhouse playing cards. They're out on the field playing flip. Their routine never changed. They were loose and they knew they were going to win."

Yount belted a first-inning home run off Palmer to get the Brewers off and running. He also added another homer, a triple and scored four runs. But the key

may have been Oglivie's sliding catch in the left field corner against pinch-hitter Joe Nolan when the game was still in doubt. Thomas added a great catch in center and Simmons cracked a two-run homer in the ninth to finish off the 10–2 win.

The Brewers were the American League East champions. It wasn't easy, but then nothing the Brewers did that year was easy.

The players may have been happier for Harvey Kuenn than they were for themselves. Kuenn was a survivor. He'd taught that to his team because he'd lived it himself. He'd had quadruple heart bypass surgery in 1976 and a year later had surgery for a stomach problem and a bowel obstruction that had led to kidney failure and uremic poisoning. More than once, doctors figured Kuenn had finally run out of time.

Then in 1980, he developed a blood clot in his right leg and had to have it amputated below the knee.

"I played 15 years in the big

(Above) Ned Yost hit one homer all season in 1982, but it was huge one, a blast in the ninth inning that beat Boston on September 28.

(Right) Bernie Brewer did a lot of sliding into the beer mug from 1978–83.

Game four of the ALCS was Mark Brouhard's moment in the sun. He knocked in three runs and tied an ALCS record by scoring four runs.

leagues and I battled every day," he said. "I figured there is no reason I couldn't battle back from this. The only way I would get beat was if I beat myself and I wasn't going to let that happen."

The next challenge that awaited Milwaukee was the California Angels, champs of the AL West — a team, like the Brewers, who had always been close, but never champions.

But in the playoff opener in Anaheim, the Angels, more specifically Don Baylor, flexed their muscles against Brewers starter Caldwell.

Baylor tied a playoff record with five RBI as California beat the Brewers 8–3. The Brewers actually led 3–2, thanks to a two-run Thomas homer off Tommy John. Then in the fourth, Baylor nailed a two-run triple as part of a four-run Angel uprising.

"We were just hoping Mike could keep us close," Cooper said. "Then that triple Baylor got really kind of stung. That really kind of put the nail in."

John went the distance for California, holding the mighty Brewers to seven hits while striking out five.

Game Two was no better for

the Brewers as journeyman pitcher Bruce Kison fired a five-hitter and struck out eight on the way to a 4–2 Angels win. The Brewers, in fact, managed to hit only five balls out of the infield against Kison.

"We were unable to get him in any kind of trouble," said a perplexed Oglivie. "The important thing for us is to put a pitcher in a spot, to put guys on base. We were unable to do that."

Kison didn't have a clue as to how he was able to handle the Brewers. "If I did," he said, "I'd apply it to the rest of the season."

The Brewers got their only two runs in the fifth inning on Molitor's inside-the-park homer. After that, there was nothing.

Once again, as they did a week earlier in Baltimore, the Brewers faced extinction. And, once again, they fought back.

Back in front of a raucous home crowd at County Stadium, Sutton struck out eight and Molitor hit a two-run homer to key a 5–3 win.

"It's fun to play when it's on the line," said Sutton. "It was on the line, and I was going to go out and enjoy myself."

Given new life, the Brewers tied

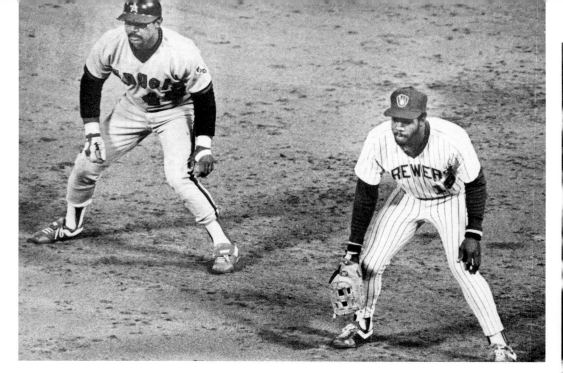

(Above) Despite being a great hitter, Oglivie will perhaps always be known for that stunning sliding catch against the Orioles in the regular-season finale.

(Left) Two of the game's best — Reggie Jackson and Cecil Cooper.

the series the next day, thanks to another unlikely hero. Mark Brouhard, subbing for the injured Oglivie, became another part of Brewers lore by scoring four runs, an ALCS record, and driving in three more in a 9–5 victory.

"I knew the only way I'd get to start in this series was if someone got hurt," said Brouhard, who played in only 60 regular season games. "I sure didn't want that to happen."

But Brouhard got the call when Oglivie crashed into a wall in the previous game and injured his ribs. It was Brouhard's first appearance in almost a month. Brouhard singled and doubled early to help give the Brewers a 7–1 lead. After a Baylor grand slam in the eighth closed the gap to 7–5, Brouhard put the game away with a two-run homer in the bottom of the inning.

After that, the 51,000 frenzied fans roared for Brouhard to give a curtain call, which he finally did. Reluctantly.

"It was pretty hard to top that

in my career," said Brouhard. "That was the highlight of my career."

All of which set up another showdown on October 10 at a gray, cool County Stadium, with the winner moving on to the first World Series appearance for its franchise.

And with another game came another hero and another struggle. The Brewers once again trailed late against the Angels, heading into the bottom of the seventh behind 3–2. And, ironically, the most important rally of the season by the most awesome offensive team in baseball started on a cue shot by right fielder Charlie Moore. Moore blooped a hit off his bat handle about 100 feet straight over the pitcher's mound.

Three Angels — shortstop Tim Foli, second baseman Bobby Grich and first baseman Rod Carew — all charged in for it and Grich dove, holding his glove up and claiming he'd caught it.

Umpires Al Clark and Larry

123

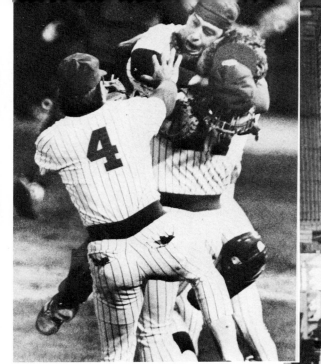

Originally a catcher, Charlie Moore was also an outstanding, and underrated, rightfielder. He made this diving catch in the playoffs and also cut down Reggie Jackson trying to take third base in Game 5 of the playoffs.

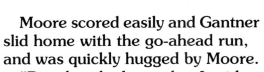

Barnett signalled Moore out, and two others, Don Denkinger and Bill Kunkel, said no, Grich had trapped the ball. Denkinger and Kunkel prevailed and Moore was safe.

Gantner followed with a single, Molitor fouled out and Yount walked. That brought up the struggling Cooper, who had only two hits in 19 at-bats in the ALCS. He'd also struck out in the fifth inning with two runners on to kill a potential rally.

"When I was on the on-deck circle, I looked up at my wife," Cooper said. "She said, 'You're going to get a hit, you're going to get a hit.' She kept telling me that."

She was right. Cooper slapped a Luis Sanchez offering into left field, motioning with his arms for the ball to get down on the ground. That pleading from Cooper is ingrained into Brewers fans the same way Red Sox fans remember Carlton Fisk pleading with his home run to stay fair in the 1975 World Series.

Moore scored easily and Gantner slid home with the go-ahead run, and was quickly hugged by Moore.

"People asked me what I said to him," Moore said. "I don't think I said anything. It just burst out of me. That was a way to let everything out."

Of course, the stadium erupted, too. "I've never heard anything like that before," said Gantner.

Lefty Bob McClure, in relief of winning pitcher Vuckovich, got the Angels out in the eighth, thanks to a leaping catch against the wall by centerfielder Marshall Edwards on a Baylor drive. Pete

Go Brewers Go!
Wallbangers win AL title

Downtown strip jumps for joy

Champs at last. Fans poured out onto Wisconsin Avenue in jubilation and Harvey Kuenn exults.

Ladd then came on in the ninth to finish up.

With two outs in the ninth and leading by a run, Ladd faced Carew, one of the great hitters of all time.

"I remember thinking that we were an out from the World Series and Rod Carew was up," said Bud Selig, who nervously puffed on his Tiparillo high above County Stadium. "Why couldn't it have been somebody else?"

But Carew hit a sharp one-hopper to Yount at short. Robin gobbled it up and threw to Cooper for the final out.

"I don't remember a whole lot but I can still picture that play in my mind," Yount said. "It was so loud, you couldn't hear anything. You could usually hear the ball hit the bat, you can hear things going on during the game. But not this time. All you did was react to the sights. I remember catching it and when I threw it, it seemed like it took five minutes for the ball to get over there. I could see it going through the air and I wasn't sure if it was ever going to get to the first baseman."

Milwaukee erupted.

Fans poured out onto the field

(Above) Paul Molitor set a World Series record with five hits in Game 1.

(Right) Mike Caldwell spun a masterful three-hit shutout in Game 1 of the World Series against the St. Louis Cardinals. He also won Game 5.

and onto the streets downtown to celebrate the Brewers as American League champions.

"I remember driving along down on Wisconsin Avenue and seeing the celebration," said Dalton. "It was a great feeling knowing that you had a little bit to do with it."

But the work wasn't finished. Not yet. There was the little matter of the World Series against the Cardinals, in a matchup already dubbed "The Suds Series" since both cities knew a thing or two about the making, and drinking, of beer.

It was almost too easy for the Brewers in the first game in St. Louis. The Cardinals had no clue against Caldwell and his devilish sinker and the Brewers pounded out 17 hits — five alone by Molitor — on their way to a 10–0 win.

"I think when you dream, you always dream about pitching a no-hitter in the seventh game,"

Caldwell said. "But right now I'll take a three-hit shutout in the first game."

Caldwell threw 15 ground ball outs and retired 17 of the first 18 hitters he faced. Darrell Porter, an ex-Brewer, had two of the Cardinals hits.

Meanwhile, the Brewers rediscovered their offense. Molitor set a World Series record with those five hits, Yount added four, including a two-run double, and Ted Simmons hit a home run, the only one of the game.

"People think we're nine lumberjacks dragging our bats out there to take three swings and hit a home run," Simmons said. "They might be surprised."

The second game was a different story and created the first true realization how much the Brewers missed the injured Fingers.

The Brewers blew a 3–0 lead, then lost the game in the eighth when the usually reliable Ladd walked pinch-hitter Steve Braun

Gorman Thomas swings . . . and it's gone!

with the bases loaded to give St. Louis the 5–4 triumph.

Ladd admitted he lost his cool when umpire Bill Haller called ball four on Lonnie Smith on a pitch that Ladd, and the rest of the Brewers, thought was strike three. That walk loaded the bases and then Ladd threw four balls that weren't even close to the strike zone against Braun.

Still, the Brewers headed home tied and ready to give Milwaukee, hosting its first World Series in 24 years, something to talk about. But it didn't quite work out as they'd planned as Cardinal fire-baller Joaquin Andujar shut down the Brewers, 6–2.

"We're holding true to form," said third base coach Harry Warner. "We're not going to do anything easy."

Vuckovich, who had been winless in his last five starts, didn't pitch badly, allowing only six hits in 8⅔

innings. But two of those were home runs by rookie Willie McGee and two others were a double and triple by Lonnie Smith.

The Brewers were able to knock Andujar out of the game — literally — when Simmons' one-hop smash in the seventh inning hit Andujar in the knee and forced him to leave. But a trio of Cardinal relievers, including Bruce Sutter, shut the door even though the Brewers threatened late.

The Brewers loaded the bases in the seventh but couldn't score. Cooper hit a two-run homer in the eighth off Sutter to pull within 5–2 and, with a man on in the ninth, Gorman Thomas hit a drive to left center that he figured was gone.

"When I hit that ball, I went into my trot right out of the box," he said. "I thought it was out."

But McGee leaped over the fence and brought the ball back

to snuff out Milwaukee's last hope.

Thomas got another chance the next day. It was a wild affair that saw the Brewers again fall behind, this time 5–1 in the seventh inning. Thomas, stuck in a 5 for 59 slump (he called it a slouch), had fouled out to the catcher twice, the second one to start off the seventh — bringing a chorus of boos from the County Stadium crowd.

"I can't remember the last time I heard that," Money said.

But the boos were hushed very, very quickly. After Thomas' out, Oglivie reached on an error and Money singled before Moore popped up for the second out. Gantner followed with an RBI double, Molitor walked to load the bases and Yount drilled a single to right to bring the Brewers within one, 5–4.

Cooper followed with a game-tying single to left, a wild pitch moved the runners up and new reliever Jeff Lahti was called on to intentionally walk Simmons.

That brought Thomas back up, and he took a 1–2 Lahti slider and drilled it to left for the two-run single that gave Milwaukee the 7–5 win.

"The first time up, I was trying to get something going," Thomas said. "The second time, I'm trying to keep it going. I started the inning with a pop up to the catcher. I guess you could say I started the winning rally."

On a chilly Sunday afternoon, the Brewers moved within a game of their first world championship when they beat the Cardinals 6–4, again behind Caldwell.

While Caldwell had cruised in the Series opener, he struggled

this time, giving up 14 hits. But he, and the Brewers, hung on.

"I'm more proud of the one I won today than the one I pitched the other day," he said. "The other night, everything went right for us. I had to work a little harder for this one."

Offensively, six Brewers drove in runs and they finished with 11 hits, four by Yount.

"Every kid dreams about playing in the World Series," Yount said. "This is better than I dreamed."

The Cardinals did make a run at Milwaukee in the ninth, scoring two off Caldwell to make the score 6–4. But the unheralded McClure struck out McGee and got pinch-hitter Gene Tenace to fly out to end the game, recording his second straight save.

So sure was Milwaukee that a world championship was headed its way, an ad appeared in the *Milwaukee Journal* trumpeting a "Brewers World Championship Plaque." It was "destined to become a valuable collector's item" and sold for $35. Then, in small type, the ad said, "In case of the very remote possibility that the Brewers do not win the series, words 'World Champions' will be replaced with 'American League Champions.'"

Game Six back in St. Louis figured to be a mismatch between the veteran Sutton and young pup John Stuper. "You have to consider it a mismatch," admitted Stuper.

It was. Stuper held the Brewers to four hits as St. Louis rolled 13–1. Stuper even returned after a two-hour, 13-minute rain delay to inflict more punishment on the visitors.

"I was more nervous than I'd

Despite falling to the Cardinals in seven games, thousands of fans turned out to honor the Brewers. The highlight had to be Robin Yount riding around County Stadium on his motorcycle.

ever been in my life," Stuper said, "but I'd say around the third or fourth inning, I got in a groove. I was sort of confident."

So, guess what? For the third time in a less than a month, it had come down to one game for the Brewers. One game. For it all.

And this time, the Cards stood up to the pressure, rallying to beat the Brewers, 6–3. The Brewers led 3–1 in the sixth but the Cards battled back to take the lead in the bottom of the sixth off Vuckovich.

Andujar went seven strong innings, Lonnie Smith scored twice and had three hits and Keith Hernandez drove in two runs to pace the winners. Darrell Porter, the ex-Brewer, was named MVP.

Yount and Molitor led the Brewers, hitting .414 and .355 respectively. Gantner and Moore also had good Series, hitting .333 and .346 respectively.

So it was over. But it was not forgotten. Milwaukee celebrated its heroes as more than 100,000 celebrants lined Wisconsin Avenue for a parade and thousands more filed into County Stadium to honor the team. The highlight came when Yount, a motorcycle fanatic, roared out from behind the left field fence on his bike and circled the stadium as the crowd erupted.

On the podium afterward, Yount said simply, "I'm not very good at making speeches, but I sure can ride a motorcycle."

"Harvey's Wallbangers" began to fade in 1983 and by the end of the season, it was clear Harvey Kuenn was on the way out. He was replaced in 1984 by 38-year-old Rene Lachemann, who had recently been canned by Seattle. Lachemann barely lasted one season.

(Right) Don Sutton and Harvey Kuenn celebrate an ALCS victory over the Angels.

"I told the players after the final game that they were world champions in my eyes and they had nothing to hang their heads about," Kuenn said. "The reception the fans gave us in Milwaukee showed us you feel the same way. It's something that could only happen in Milwaukee."

But while players made brave predictions that 1983 would be "the" year, it wasn't. In fact, Harvey's Wallbangers were already starting to sputter.

It started in spring training with the loss of Vuckovich and Fingers to injury. In all, eight key players would miss playing time, including Yount, Moose Haas and Oglivie.

The Brewers struggled early, limping to a 35–36 record through June. But in July and August, they caught fire, going 40–21 and surging into first place on August 25. That was the last time they'd see it. Exhausted from getting back into contention, the Brewers bats fell silent and the offense disappeared. They had a disastrous West Coast road trip, going 3–8. Then they went on a 10-game losing skid in September.

"We'd given so much getting back into the race, there was nothing left in September," Yount admitted.

The Brewers lost 18 of their final 30 games and eventually toppled to fifth in the AL East, even though they posted another solid record of 87–75, their sixth straight winning season.

Cooper had another incredible season, hitting .307 and tying for the league lead in RBI with 126 despite playing only 106 games.

The Brewers also set an all-time attendance record as 2,397,131 fans, third best in baseball and an average of more than 31,000 per game, crammed into County Stadium.

But it was becoming clear that Harvey's Wallbangers were beginning to fade. At the end of the '83 season, Dalton replaced Kuenn with 38-year-old wonderboy Rene Lachemann, who had been fired earlier that season by Seattle.

"It was very tough to fire Harvey," Dalton said. "My heart couldn't do it but my head had to. I felt after '83 the club was drifting away and something had to be done. It was a very, very difficult decision."

The dismantling really started earlier that season when Thomas and pitcher Jamie Easterly were sent to Cleveland for pitcher Rick Waits and outfielder Rick Manning. The move crushed Thomas and Brewers fans, but it was a move that had to be made, according to Dalton.

Three years later, the Brewers re-signed Thomas and his first game back in Milwaukee, there were nearly 38,000 fans on hand to watch a meaningless Monday night game with the Yankees.

Oglivie moved on, too, leaving the Brewers in 1985 and playing a year in Japan before retiring. He now coaches in the Brewer minor league system. And Cooper, perhaps the best all-around hitter in franchise history, retired in 1987, finishing in the top five all-time in 13 team offensive categories.

Molitor, Gantner and Yount, of course, stayed on to see what new adventures awaited the Brewers.

And there were plenty. ❖

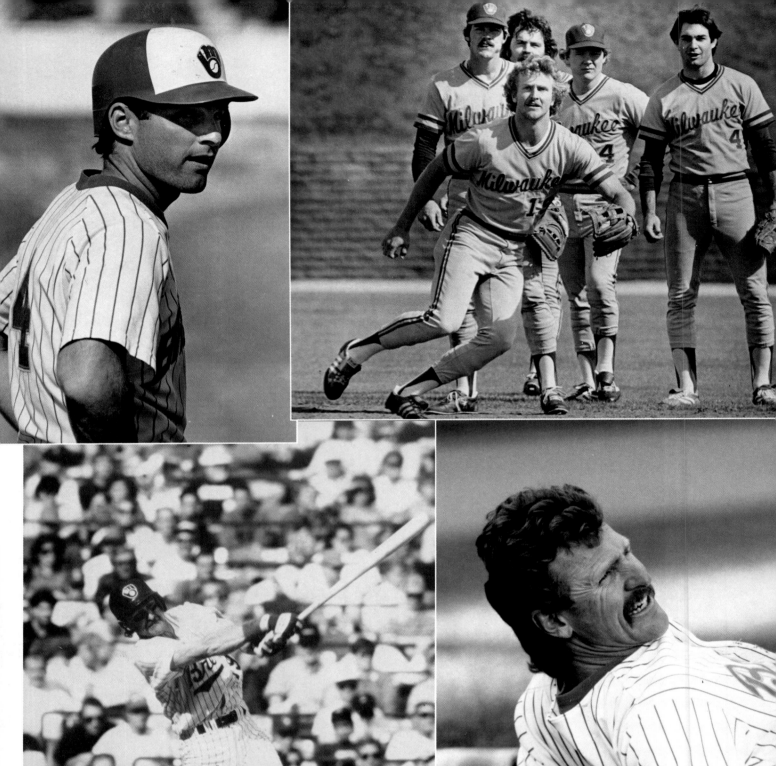
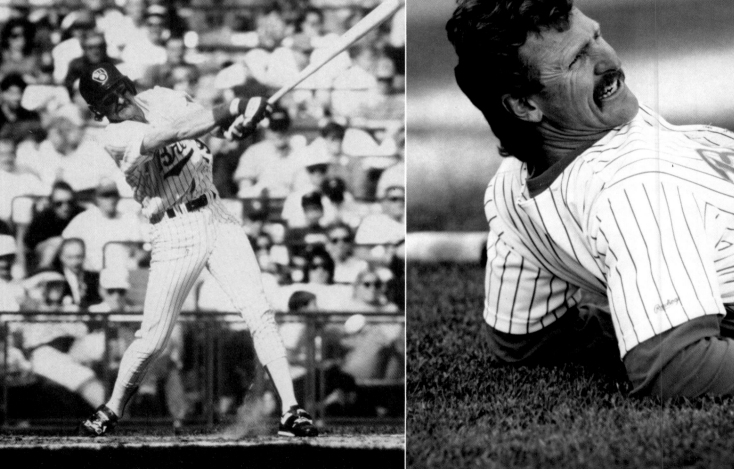

Chapter Four

Molly, Gumby and The Kid

THEY WERE THE FIRST ONES OUT TO GREET "The Kid." They had to be. It was fitting. It was perfect. It seemed the only way things could be.

So on a muggy September night in 1992, when Robin Yount had taken his place in baseball's pantheon with his 3,000th hit, there they were, joining their long-time buddy at first base.

Paul Molitor, Jim Gantner and Robin Yount standing on first base, hugging. Together. Again. Just as it should be.

It lasted only a moment, though, as the rest of the Brewers joined the celebration. But it proved to be a poignant moment for three of the most enduring players in Milwaukee baseball history. As it turned out, that short, emotional gathering at first base would really be the last time those three were together in Brewers uniforms.

Molly, Gumby and The Kid.

They were three distinct personalities playing three very distinct brands of baseball and thrown together at just the right point in history for a team that desperately needed each of them and the special talents they possessed.

The entire Brewers team came out to honor Robin Yount after his 3,000th hit in 1992, but the first two to greet him were Jim Gantner and Paul Molitor.

(Above) Paul Molitor played 15 seasons in Milwaukee and is among the club's all-time leaders in just about every offensive category.

(Right) After a shoulder injury forced Robin Yount out at shortstop, he moved to centerfield, where he excelled as well.

Molly, Gumby and The Kid.

Among them, they played 6,386 games together, scored 3,571 runs, knocked in 2,714 runs combined for 6,399 hits and triggered about a million memories.

"You don't realize how much you'll miss guys until they're gone," said long-time radio broadcaster Bob Uecker. "It would have been nice for this trio to play together until their last game. But it didn't happen that way. It usually doesn't. The kind of numbers Paul put up are amazing. He never popped off. He did his job. If he was in New York or Los Angeles or Chicago and had his 39-game hitting streak, it would have been unbelieveable. The hype. The media.

"He never complained about publicity. He wanted it that way. He loved it. Jimmy is a perfect example of how hard work pays off. He may not have had the same tools as Paulie or Robin, but when it comes to heart and guts, no one is better. Any major league manager who had to manage against these guys would tell you that they would love to have

a roster filled with players like Robin, Paul and Jimmy. Players like that don't come around very often."

It will never be seen again, either. Not with baseball's current transient nature. Players change teams like shirts, discarding one for another at a moment's notice.

Loyalty? Please. Commitment? Thanks, anyway. Today, baseball is a game of nomads.

Molly, Gumby and The Kid.

But it wasn't always that way. No, there was a time when the team you played for meant almost as much as the game itself. A time when you figured the team you signed with as an 18-year-old stripling was the same team you'd end your career with.

It happened. At least it used to.

Molly, Gumby and The Kid.

The Milwaukee Brewers know a little something about that. They know what it took to keep players together, to keep some continuity, to keep things together.

It is no coincidence that in the years Paul Molitor, Jim Gantner and Robin Yount played together on the same field, the Brewers were one of baseball's most consistent teams.

Molly — Paul Molitor — was the gregarious one. He was eloquent and friendly and helpful to confused sports writers who'd roam the clubhouse looking for a friendly face or a decent quote. He always made time for fans, whether they wanted an autograph or a photo or just to say hello. He loved his role with the Brewers and he played it to the hilt. In return, he earned a spot as one of the all-time favorites of Brewers fans.

Gumby — Jim Gantner — was the scrappy little battler. Never blessed with a lot of natural baseball skills, he still worked his tail off every year and was always there when he was needed. He was a Wisconsin kid who wanted nothing more than a chance to prove himself. And did.

The Kid — Robin Yount — is, well, Robin Yount. Still called by that nickname even though he's pushing 40, Yount has become the embodiment of the Brewers. Quiet, resolute, he has always let his play do his talking for him.

Yount has played for the Brewers 20 years, Gantner played 15 years and Molitor, before signing with the Toronto Blue Jays prior to the 1993 season, had 15 years invested with the Brewers.

Think about that. Three players who put in a combined 52 years for one team. Unheard of these days.

"I doubt that it will ever happen again in baseball," Gantner said. "Three guys on the same team for 15 years? A lot of guys won't even play that long. It's just been a privilege for me to play with two Hall of Famers — at least Paulie

should be a Hall of Famer. It was great."

It wasn't always easy and it certainly wasn't always a picnic, but it was one heck of a ride anyway. There was Yount, first at shortstop and then in centerfield; Gantner, rock solid at second base, third base and shortstop; and Molitor, a third baseman, a shortstop, a second baseman, an outfielder, a first baseman. Actually he did almost anything that was needed.

And together they helped bring the Milwaukee Brewers into the upper echelons of baseball.

Jim Gantner spent a lot of time in mid-air and was known as one of the game's best in making the double play pivot from second base.

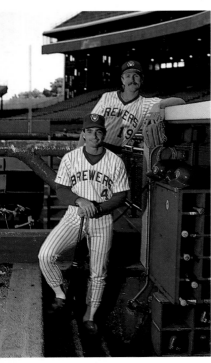

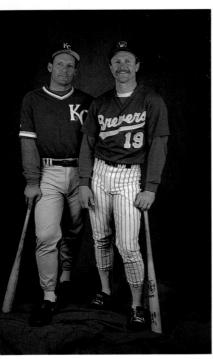

For so long, they have been linked together, almost lacking individual identities. It was always Yount-Molitor-Gantner or some variation of the theme. But they were very different people, very different players. So let's break up the set and give each of them their due.

ROBIN YOUNT: They have run out of superlatives to describe Robin Yount.

Bud Selig: "My daughters always kidded me because I always told them Robin was the kind of person I'd always wanted them to marry. He's just a wonderful young man."

Sal Bando: "He plays the game the way it was meant to be played."

George Bamberger: "I can't say enough about him. He always gave 100 percent and never, ever complained. He's a real professional."

Harry Dalton: "The ultimate professional and a cinch Hall of Famer."

Robin Yount: "I'm nothing special."

Hmmm.

That, you see, is typical. Yount can be maddeningly modest until you realize that it's just the way he is. He knows no other way to be. While everyone around him will trumpet his accomplishments, his career, his life, Yount simply shrugs it off as if it's really no big deal. And to him, maybe it isn't.

But his numbers say otherwise. First and foremost, he's only one of 19 players to reach the 3,000-hit plateau, and the third youngest in history at 36 years, 11 months and 24 days. He was only the second player (along with a guy named Willie Mays) to

record 3,000 hits, 200 homers, 200 stolen bases and 100 triples in his career. He is only the third player, along with Stan Musial and Hank Greenberg, to earn league most valuable player honors at two different positions — shortstop and center field, perhaps the two toughest spots on the field.

Yount is the all-time team leader in just about every offensive category and among baseball's enduring greats in many others.

And he still, even now, doesn't quite grasp what all the ruckus is about. His version of events is simple and concise. Well, heck, he says, if anybody had played as long as I have, they'd get 3,000 hits, too.

"I'm just a human being gifted with the ability to play baseball," he said.

Robin was one of those players. One of those rare, gifted types who was good at anything he tried.

"A Robin Yount triple is one of the most exciting things in baseball," said Tom Skibosh, the Brewers director of media relations.

So maybe it isn't that big a deal to him. Yount was the third player taken in the 1973 draft, behind pitcher David Clyde (to Texas) and catcher John Stearns (to Philadelphia). Clyde was rushed to the majors too quickly, developed arm problems and was out of baseball in five years. Stearns played 11 big-league seasons and no one's really quite sure what he did or where he did it.

But everyone knows about Yount, despite his almost fanatical attempts to keep his privacy. He played all of 64 games in the minors leagues before being called up in 1974 to be the Brewers short-stop of the future. Period.

He was only 18, but so what? The Kid had to learn sometime.

"I probably need more experience," said a fresh-faced Yount back in 1974, "and the best way of getting it is in the majors. That's the highest you can get and if you're going to go through it every day, that's the place to learn."

On his first big league chance, with eventual teammate Cecil Cooper on first, Yount gobbled up a grounder off the bat of Boston's Carl Yastrzemski, raced to the bag for the putout and then threw wide to first baseman George Scott.

"I remember Cecil came into second really hard," Yount recalled so many years later. "Really hard."

His first season was cut short by an injury and his second year was another learning experience as he made 44 errors, a Brewers record that still stands. But he learned. He learned a lot.

He picked up his first major league hit on April 12, 1974, a single up the middle off Baltimore's Dave McNally. For the season, he hit a respectable .250 and played as solid a shortstop as a kid two years out of high school could play. He did, however, miss the final six weeks of the season with an ankle injury.

But even back then, Yount was obsessed with winning. Personal numbers, personal achievements meant nothing to him and still don't. Winning was the only thing that concerned him and if he played well as a result, so much the better. That's why, in the spring of 1978, Yount was having

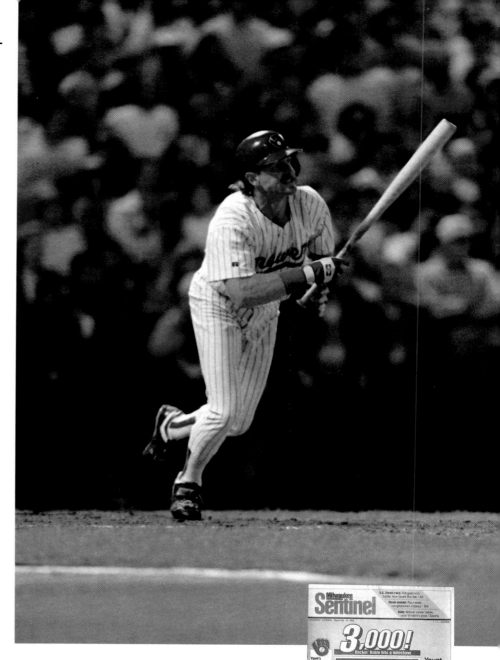

second thoughts about major league baseball. He was hobbled by an injured ankle suffered during an off-season motorcycle accident plus, through his first four seasons, the Brewers were simply a bad ballclub, having finished no higher than fifth.

"The combination made me wonder if that was really what I wanted to do," he said. "It wasn't that exciting finishing fifth or sixth every year. That didn't do a whole lot for me."

Robin Yount as a fresh-faced rookie, as an MVP in 1982 and as Hall of Famer in waiting today.

So the rumor, which Harry Dalton thinks was started by the media, was that Robin would give up baseball and take a crack at the professional golf tour.

Yount just smiles when he thinks about that.

"There aren't a whole lot of five-handicappers in the PGA Tour," he said.

Plus, in 1978, the Brewers finally began to win and Yount's interest was rekindled. With a new powerful lineup, Yount became an offensive threat himself.

"There was no one in our lineup that pitchers could pitch around," he said. "We had some pretty big thumpers in that lineup and that made everybody a better hitter."

By 1982, Yount had reached the considerable potential everyone had expected. He hit over .300 for the first time in his career, he led the league in hits and doubles and was up among the league leaders in RBI, homers, triples, slugging percentage and

total bases. He also won a Gold Glove and was named the American League MVP. He also hit better than .400 in the World Series and probably would have won that MVP honor, too, if the Brewers had won.

If the Brewers had won. Ah, there's the perceived rub. The one unattained goal, the Holy Grail that remains out of Yount's reach. He still doesn't have that World Series ring he so covets, the one item missing from his resume that would make his career complete. Yes, that thought still eats away at him at times, but not as much as it used to and not as much as people might think. That's especially true considering how things happened in 1982, with a final-game win over Baltimore to clinch the American League East, a final-game victory over California to win the AL pennant and a final-game loss to the St. Louis Cardinals in the World Series.

"We didn't win the World Series, but the way that season went, I don't think the feeling you get (as world champions) would've been any different than what we had experienced two times earlier within a couple of weeks," he said. "Winning the World Series would have been that feeling a third time."

The same feeling surrounded his quest to reach 3,000 hits. It is perhaps the perfect irony that one of baseball's most talked-about milestones was being pursued by one of baseball's most private men. As he neared the 3,000 mark in late August and early September 1992, the constant media barrage was far more than he wanted to deal with.

But deal with it he did, reluctantly. Again, he didn't see what all the fuss was about.

"If you play long enough, you're going to get there," he said. "It's that simple. You don't have to be great to get 3,000 hits. You've got to be good enough to stay in the lineup but you definitely don't have to be great."

Still, there was a new excitement at County Stadium as the Brewers, hip-deep in a pennant race, were also keeping an eye on Yount and his impending record. And somewhat out of character, he made it tough on everyone involved.

Actually, there was some question if Yount would even reach 3,000 hits in '92, since he'd been mired in an almost season-long hitting slump. But he went on a tear in late July, carrying him to the threshold of the coveted three grand. The Brewers came home for a three-game homestand against the Cleveland Indians and

Yount stood three hits shy of the magic mark.

Even by that stage, Yount was firmly convinced he wasn't doing anything particularly noteworthy. As a result, he threatened, probably only half jokingly, that he was going to hit a home run for No. 3,000 so he wouldn't have to stand on base and acknowledge an honor that clearly made him uncomfortable.

"I've never looked at myself as a great ballplayer," he said. "I don't know what's so great about a .280 (actually .288) lifetime hitter. But it's been good enough to keep my name in the lineup. I just can't wait for this to end."

Robin Yount came up as an 18-year-old short-stop, where he set a club record for errors that still stands today.

The first game, with 41,000 fans on hand, he scorched a single to right off Dennis Cook. The next night, he singled off Jack Armstrong with another 40,000 watching. That set the stage for the series finale September 9.

With a crowd of 47,589 on hand, Yount did something he rarely did — he got caught up in the hype. After all the denials, even Yount was beginning to understand how much this meant to the fans of Milwaukee and, if he dared admit it, to himself as well.

"I really, really wanted to see it happen at home," he said. "Maybe I wanted to see it happen too much and I got pretty caught up in it."

As a result, Yount went hitless in three tries against Indians pitcher Jose Mesa and the unthinkable was appearing more likely. Yount would wind up getting his milestone hit on the road. It was too awful to contemplate.

Then he stepped up in the seventh inning for what figured to be his final at-bat. The crowd stood and pleaded. After fouling off one pitch, he drilled a no-doubt-about-it single to right-center, sending the stadium into convulsions.

The first ones to greet Yount at first base were his old pals, Jim Gantner and Paul Molitor.

"I remember coming back to first base and seeing Jim and Paulie standing on the bag," said Yount. "It was a very exciting moment in my career."

"There are a few moments in baseball I won't forget, and that's one of them," said Gantner. "It was just a great moment. There wasn't too much said between the three of us because the emotional level was so high. But there was a lot of hugging. I was pretty choked up."

"The tears were flowing," Molitor said. "I was pretty numb going up there. He gave us the biggest bear hugs and on a normal day, Robin would fight at being picked up."

And while he maintained to the last that it was just another hit, even he had to concede it was a pretty special hit.

"The way the fans got into the whole thing here and all the excitement behind it, it really turned into a lot more than I was thinking it was ever going to be."

As Yount stood on first base saluting the crowd, a five-minute ovation ensued and even the stoic one began to crack, just a little.

"This is special," he admitted.

It's now a running joke in the County Stadium press box that every time Yount steps to the plate, or takes a swing, or does anything on the diamond, it puts him that much higher on the all-time baseball list.

There are times when first base coach Tim Foli will clip the daily "Yount Count" from media notes and put them under his hat. When Yount reaches first base, Foli brings out the sheet and begins to recite just who he passed or tied on the career lists with that hit, or walk or at-bat.

"I usually have to tell him to shut up," Yount said.

Yes, they have run out of things to say about Robin Yount. It is no longer a marvel that he switched from shortstop to center field in 1985 because of recurring shoulder problems and would go on to win an MVP award in 1989 playing there.

"I try to play hard every day and play as many games as I can," he said. "That's all I can do. I didn't ever play the game trying to get 3,000 hits. I would've been just as happy getting 1,000 hits. I get satisfaction from going on the field and doing what it takes to beat the opponent that particular game. I don't get satisfaction from seeing how high I can get my name on a list. That doesn't do anything for me.

"But getting a hit to win a game, that does something for me. I could be 0 for 10, but if I

get a hit to win that game, that feels pretty good. But going 4 for 4 and getting your 3,000th hit in the meantime and losing the game, well, that's not what I go out there for."

Someday, the Brewers will have to accept life without Robin Yount. It is, to many, as unimaginable as Christmas without Santa Claus. But it is inevitable. His plan has been to stick around for one more shot at winning a World Series, but time has been running out and Yount knows it.

"But even if I don't win a World Series, I've had a good career," he said.

Jimmy Gantner was known as an outstanding fielder in his 15 years with the Brewers.

Yount will ride off into the sunset on his motorcycle, the only other passion he has besides baseball. He will ride off and never look back. There will be no reason to. The quiet Californian who always let his play do the talking, did what he could with what he had and that's always been enough.

"Robin Yount is everything that's great about the Brewers," said Bamberger. "There will never be another one like him."

JIM GANTNER: A man with a dream. From the time he was a kid in his native Eden, Wisconsin, 40 miles north of Milwaukee, Gantner would pretend he was a member of his favorite team, the Milwaukee Braves.

"Henry Aaron and Eddie Mathews were my heroes when I was a kid," he said. "I remember throwing the ball up against my garage and pretending I was playing with Henry Aaron."

Fast forward to 1976 and the final game of another lost season for the Brewers. On a warm Sunday afternoon at County Stadium, Aaron reaches base on his last at-bat ever and Gantner, just called up from the minors, goes in as a pinch-runner. Gantner has died and gone to heaven.

"That's something I can tell my granchildren, though they may not believe me," Gantner said. "I'm running for one of my childhood heroes."

This is the guy they call Gumby. Gantner has always viewed major league baseball with just a little bit of awe. Yes, he played for 15 seasons through 1992 and was one of the American League's best second basemen in that time. But for some reason, he was never quite sure if he fit in.

"Jim was a self-made big leaguer," Yount said. "He didn't have the tools that 99 percent of the people in the big leagues had, yet, because of his mental toughness and his heart, he was able to compete and do an outstanding job at the major league level on a regular basis. He did it with guts."

It's a characterization Gantner won't argue with.

"I grew up in a big family so nothing was given to you," he said. "You worked for what you got. That was my attitude: Take nothing for granted and keep going hard."

It was the way Gantner played every day, on every play — the only way he knew how to play the game.

He was no baseball prodigy, not like Yount and not like Molitor, both of whom were destined for stardom. But he did share one trait — the realization that baseball was what he wanted to do for a living.

"That was something that was in my heart from the time I was six years old," Gantner said. "I had no idea what I wanted to do if I didn't make it in baseball."

But he did. Of course, it wasn't easy, but he made it.

Gantner got his first real shot in college, playing for the burgeoning Division III baseball powerhouse at the University of Wisconsin-Oshkosh. After two seasons there, he was a 12th-round draft pick of the Brewers in 1974.

"I was just looking for a chance to get into pro baseball," he said. "All I wanted was that chance."

Gantner's doggedness, and his ability to play any infield position, made him a valuable commodity and, in 1976, he got called up to the big club for the final month of the season. His first big league hit came on September 3 when he singled off Detroit hotshot rookie Mark Fidrych.

"That was the same game Mike Hegan hit for the cycle," Gantner said. "I remember we beat Fidrych real bad. That's one game you don't forget."

Gantner got another brief look in 1977, but at spring training in 1978, he seized his first real opportunity.

"Harry Dalton said that since we finished 32 games out of first in 1977, nobody's going to be guaranteed a job. He knew I couldn't become a starter in '78 because there were too many guys ahead of me. But if I could prove to George Bamberger that I could play all infield positions, I had a chance to make the team as a utility player."

"He was one of those guys that surprised me," Dalton said. "He came out of our minor league system and we thought he'd be a big leaguer, but nothing like what he became."

Eventually, Gantner would become another critical component the Brewers needed to become competitive. By 1981, the Brewers decided it was time to find a permanent spot for Gantner so manager Buck Rodgers installed him at second, moved Molitor to center and switched regular centerfielder Gorman Thomas to right, a move that infuriated Thomas.

Eventually, Thomas moved back to center and Molitor became a third baseman. But Gantner stayed at second. And didn't budge for nearly a decade, earning the distinction as having the longest stint at second base in Milwaukee baseball history — Brewers or Braves.

Gantner admitted there was some early pressure being a Wisconsin boy playing for the home-state team.

"The first couple of years, I wished I could've started with another team because there was too much outside pressure," he

Call it Gumby's Memorial. Jim Gantner suffered a season-ending injury to his left knee during an August 1989 collision at second base with New York Yankees rookie Marcus Lawton. In tribute to Gantner, the Brewers put Gumby's batting helmet on the Gatorade cooler before every game.

Jim Gantner made his first appearance in Milwaukee in 1976 but stayed for good in 1978, where he became one of baseball's top second basemen.

the league in chances three different years — 1981, 1983 and 1984.

"I was hoping to just maybe get 10 years in," Gantner said. "It's out of your control, but you hope to stay healthy and you want to play every day. That's what I wanted to accomplish."

Gantner stayed relatively free of injury until 1989, when he suffered a serious knee injury. But he battled back, reclaimed his starting job, hit .283 (his highest mark since 1982) and was named the Brewers comeback player of the year in 1990.

The underdog, the guy with limited talent but a heart the size of County Stadium, reached his goal. Gantner wanted to play 10 years and he played 15.

And he made a difference. A big difference.

said. "People wanted your time and we didn't want to say no. But after a while, the notoriety wears off and it's great to play in your home state."

Gantner still lives in Wisconsin with his family. "When the season's over, we're home," he said.

Never an offensive juggernaut, Gantner nonetheless posted some decent numbers when needed. He hit a career-best .295 in 1982 — up to .333 in the World Series — and in 1983 followed it up with a .282 average, 11 home runs and 74 RBI. For his career, he finished with a .274 average, played in 1,801 games and had 1,696 hits.

But it wasn't at the plate where Gantner was most valuable. His forte was defense and he played second base with the best of them. Better, in fact. His career .992 fielding percentage is the all-time best for second basemen in the American League. He also led

PAUL MOLITOR: They never got to tell Paul Molitor how much they loved him. How much they respected him. How much he meant to them.

How much they missed him.

Brewers fans finally got that chance June 25, 1993, when Molly came home. To County Stadium, where he belonged. Where he really, truly belonged.

But it was different. Paul Molitor, the Ignitor, the guy you expected to be a Brewers player until Milwaukee fell into Lake Michigan, was wearing a Toronto Blue Jays uniform. And it looked so queer, so odd. Like painting a moustache on the Mona Lisa. It just wasn't right, but there it was anyway — since he'd left via free agency following the 1992 season.

Despite some serious mixed feelings, Brewers fans, perhaps

Paul Molitor is the Brewers' all-time leader in stolen bases with 412.

the most forgiving and understanding in baseball, rose. They couldn't help it. They had to. This was Molly.

So some 40,000 patrons got to their feet and cheered one of the most beloved players in Brewers history as he stepped to the plate in the first inning.

"I just didn't want to cry," Molitor said. "My wife was really worried about that because she knows how I can be."

He tipped his batting helmet, took a deep breath, stepped into the batter's box and slapped an RBI single to center.

Figures, right?

He did the same thing for 15 years with the Brewers. Whether he played first base or the outfield, shortstop or third base or was the designated hitter, Molitor seemingly always delivered when the Brewers needed it most.

Someone, somewhere, tagged him with that horrid Ignitor nickname, which he tries to ignore whenever possible. "When I come in the room, no one says, "Hey everybody, here comes The Ignitor," he said with a laugh.

But while he understandably despises the name, it does fit.

Wherever Paul Molitor played, he excelled, be it at shortstop, third base, first base or the outfield.

Like a glove. He ignited so many rallies in his years in Milwaukee that it became almost commonplace, and it certainly was expected. Since 1978, when he broke into the bigs as a first-round draft pick fresh off a stellar collegiate career at the University of Minnesota, the Brewers won nearly 55 percent of their games when he was in the lineup. When he wasn't, they won only 45 percent.

The numbers don't lie. That's what Molitor meant to the Brewers. In his career with the Brewers, he played every position except pitcher and catcher and had he stayed, who knows?

He was a .303 career hitter, he scored 1,275 runs, pounded out 2,281 hits and would lead the Brewers in just about every offensive category if not for that guy named Yount.

Molly was a five-time All-Star, the American League rookie of the year in 1978, is one of four Brewers to hit for the cycle and had three stolen bases in one inning, tying a league record. He also set a World Series record with five hits in one game and hit three home runs in a game.

And, oh yes, wasn't there something about a 39-game hitting streak?

"You could tell he was going to be a star," said Dee Fondy, who scouted and signed Molitor out of college. "You just knew it."

Molitor was a lot like Yount in that regard. He was the third player taken in the 1977 June draft, just as Yount had been four years earlier. Molly had the talent, the look of a star. Like Yount, he only played in 64 minor league games and was the Brewers starting shortstop opening day 1978 when, ironically, Yount was hurt.

But unlike Yount, who has managed a relatively injury-free career, Molitor was plagued for years by various ailments ranging from nagging things to downright serious problems. In all, injuries cost Molitor more than 500 games.

Molitor has accepted the bad breaks with typical aplomb.

"I've learned that with each injury and each stint on the disabled list, that you can't have regrets," he said. "Naturally, you ponder what might have been. But if you think about it all the time, it can be counterproductive. You can never get them back. I'm just thankful for what I've been able to do with my career and that I'm still fortunate enough to be playing. Hopefully, I'll stay healthy."

And that's the strange part. As Molitor has gotten older, at the time when injuries should be increasing, he has been his healthiest as time's gone by.

In 1991, Molitor had perhaps his best all-around season, hitting .325 and leading the majors in hits (216) and runs (133). In '92, when the Brewers were making an unexpected run at the AL East title, Molitor was at his best. He played in 158 games, led the Brewers in batting average (.320), hits (195), at-bats (609) and RBI (89) and was second in runs scored with 89.

But to paraphrase a popular bumper sticker, stuff happens.

And a lot of stuff happened during Molitor's contract negotiations after the '92 season. Faced with a contract demand the Brewers simply couldn't match, the unthinkable happened. Molitor signed with AL East foe Toronto.

"I never really wanted to leave," Molitor said. But when the Blue Jays offered him a four-year, $13 million deal, how could he refuse?

And the Brewers players didn't blame him. "It was a great opportunity," said Yount. "He had to take it."

No, Molitor no longer ignites Brewers rallies, but he does ignite memories. So many memories.

Obviously, the one that tops the list came in 1987, when he threatened to disturb one of baseball's most honored marks — the seemingly untouchable 56-game hitting streak of Joe DiMaggio in 1941.

In truth, Molitor never really got

that close to DiMaggio's mark, but for quite awhile, his performance had all of baseball buzzing. "Looking back, it was a lot of fun," Molitor said.

At the time, though . . .

Constantly hounded by media, Molitor only made matters worse by being so darned obliging with writers and TV people and radio types. If anybody needed a question answered, he'd take care of it.

The streak started on July 16 — ironically, the very day he returned from 44 days on the disabled list due to a hamstring injury. During the streak, which finally ended August 26, he hit .415, with

Paul Molitor gets mobbed after another game-winning hit.

149

68 hits, 7 home runs, 33 runs batted in and 15 stolen bases. It was the fifth-longest hitting streak in baseball history and was kept alive in all manner of ways — from first-inning singles to home runs in his final at-bat.

"He's one of the most exciting offensive players I've ever seen," said Harry Dalton.

"He's a Rod Carew with power," said Yount.

Molitor was as much a part of the Brewers as Yount or Selig or County Stadium. That's why his loss so shocked the fans of Milwaukee. It seemed he'd be here forever.

But in an age of skyrocketing salaries, the Brewers, in one of baseball's smallest markets, simply could not compete. "If there had been extra money, do you know what Bud Selig would have done with it?" asked current manager Phil Garner. "He would've given it to Paul Molitor."

Yet history is history and Molitor will likely finish his playing career in Toronto.

On his first visit back to Milwaukee, Molitor and Selig had a long talk. They talked about everything and they talked about nothing at all. They skirted over sensitive subjects since, well, there was no point in crying over spilled milk. But one thing they did talk about was Molitor eventually coming back to Milwaukee as a coach.

"He said he'd still like me back," said Molitor. "And I'd like that, too."

So who knows? Maybe in another five years, after Robin Yount, Paul Molitor and Jim Gantner have finally and officially hung them up, maybe they will all gather back at County Stadium as coaches for their old team. And maybe they'll think back to that first year in 1978 when all three of them were together for the first time. They will recount all those early years, the triumphs, the failures, the lives they spent together.

Then, finally, maybe they'll remember that September night in 1992 when they hugged and cried and celebrated for the last time.

And they will smile and remember how worthwhile it all was. ❖

A Cast of Characters

MILWAUKEE HAD NEVER SEEN ANYBODY like him.

Never.

Not when the Braves were still in town and certainly not with the Brewers. No way. This guy was different from anything the city had ever experienced.

He was the Boomer and that was all that needed to be said. And Milwaukee opened its arms to the biggest and best and brashest player the franchise had ever seen.

They needed him, there was no doubt about that. The Brewers had been essentially a faceless bunch in their initial years. Flashes in the pan, nice guys, marginal talents who tried like the devil but, well, you know.

But George Scott was different.

Boomer gave the Brewers an edge, a personality. He gave them their first, bona fide, God-what-is-he-going-to-say-next character. At first blush, it would seem the Brewers franchise was made up exclusively of choirboys with straight teeth and good table manners. And to be sure,

Mike Caldwell won 22 games in 1978 and was named the American League Comeback Player of the Year. Notice Caldwell's hat. He was so superstitious that he kept the same hat the entire season for fear that if he changed to a clean one, it would wreck his good fortune.

there were a few like Robin Yount and Paul Molitor and Dan Plesac and Danny Walton — guys you wanted to bring home to mother.

Scratch the surface, though, and you'll find a franchise chock full of guys with strange and wonderful talents — and not necessarily all on the baseball diamond. There was Gorman Thomas and Mike "Mr. Warmth" Caldwell. Scott and Pete Vuckovich. Gary Sheffield and Rollie Fingers and George Bamberger. What they all shared was a lot of talent.

But The Boomer was the first. He roared into Milwaukee in 1972 as part of the trade that sent popular Tommy Harper and pitchers Lew Krausse and Marty Pattin plus a minor leaguer, Pat Skrable, to Boston for Billy Conigliaro, Joe Lahoud, Jim Lonborg, Ken Brett, Don Pavletich and Scott. Make no mistake: Scott was clearly the marquee player of the group.

Boomer brought with him

phrases that might as well have been Martian to Milwaukee Brewers fans. He called his home runs "taters," his first baseman's glove he named "Black Beauty" and when asked what kind of beads he wore around his neck, Scott simply replied that they were second basemen's teeth.

The best part for Brewers fans was that Scott could still play, too. He wasn't some washed-up hanger-on pathetically trying to keep his career going by saying outrageous things. He became the Brewers' first consistent home run threat, he drove in runs and he played an unparalleled first base. As a result, he could say whatever he darned well pleased.

In 1973, when a Boston sportswriter commented that Scott was beginning to add some excess baggage around the middle, Scott just scowled and said he would work the weight off against the Red Sox pitching staff that night. During another game in '73, Yankees pitcher Sam McDowell

walked Davey May intentionally to load the bases and bring Scott to the plate. He promptly deposited a McDowell fastball two rows from the top of the left field bleachers. While rounding the bases, Scott shook his finger at McDowell, admonishing him for taking the Boomer so lightly.

In 1974, Scott, the savvy first baseman, tried to take advantage of Herb Washington, a speedy but untested Oakland A's baserunner.

"Get off the bag for a second," said Scott. "I have to clean it."

Washington was ready to oblige when he looked in Scott's glove and saw the ball. Washington smiled, called time and got off the bag.

In yet another 1973 game, Scott belted his first career grand slam to help beat the Yankees. When he took his spot at first base the next inning, the County Stadium crowd of 32,436 erupted. Even Scott was moved by that.

"It was quite a thrill for me," he said. "The main thing in playing ball is that a player likes for the fans to appreciate him. I think they appreciate me."

Brewers president Bud Selig said: "It was the greatest applause for a player I've ever heard at the stadium. I can't recall one for Henry Aaron that was as loud as that."

But Scott was more than just a good quote. Scott was the conscience for a young, inexperienced team. When they screwed up — and in those early days they screwed up a lot — Scott was there to let them know it and to point them in the right direction.

Once when the Brewers and Angels were locked in a late-inning tie and California had Ken

Berry on third base, a pop fly was lifted to short center field. In Little League, players are taught that, whenever possible, the center fielder should take the ball. But rookie Tim Johnson, the shortstop before Yount (there's a trivia question for you) called for the ball and caught it.

Johnson's momentum took him away from the infield and Berry tagged up and scored.

This, it must be understood, did not please the Boomer. He railed on and on about stupid baseball and concluded by saying, "Win the bleeping pennant? My bleep."

Or words to that effect.

It's probably safe to assume that Johnson never called off an outfielder for a pop fly again before he eventually slipped into baseball obscurity.

Yet Scott also knew when to come to his teammates' defense. In a 1974 game against the Minnesota Twins, Brewers Bobby Coluccio was beaned by Twins pitcher Ray Corbin. Furious and dazed, Coluccio headed toward the mound to confront Corbin, then stumbled and fell. That's when all hell broke loose, led, of course, by George Scott, who had

(Above) Gorman Thomas became a team leader not only on the field, but off, and was credited for sticking many Brewers with nicknames that still hang on today.

(Left) Kurt Bevacqua may not have done much on the field for the Brewers, but he's among the all-time greats in clowning.

157

George Scott was perhaps the first real character to play for the Brewers. The unpredictable first baseman always spoke his mind and never much cared who listened. Around his neck is the celebrated necklace he claimed were "second basemen's teeth."

received his own share of chin music throughout the series.

Minnesota catcher Phil Roof said of Scott: "He just went bananas."

"Every time we start to have a couple of good days, they start throwing high and tight at us," Scott said. "If our pitchers aren't going to take care of that, we will."

Thoroughly convinced the Twins were throwing at him and the rest of the Brewers, Scott went right to the top during the brawl — to Twins manager Frank Quilici, the man Scott was certain had started the trouble.

"I'm not going to work up from the bottom to get to the top," Scott fumed. "I'm going right to the top — the guy who is responsible."

Scott was so enraged during that brawl that he even tangled with his own manager, Del Crandall, in an apparent effort to get back at Quilici.

"My left side still hurts from an elbow I caught there," Crandall laughed afterward. "I could have gotten away, but my hand was stuck in one of his sleeves."

And, oh yes, the Brewers won the game.

Scott could be moody and surly and thoroughly unpleasant to be around, but he had his moments. And he could also play. His first season with the Brewers, Scott hit only .266, but he belted 20 home runs and knocked in 88 runs, fourth best in the American League. He was even better the next year, hitting .306 and driving home 107 runs.

Perhaps his best season was 1975, his next to last full year with the Brewers. With newly acquired Henry Aaron, the all-time home run champ, hitting behind him, Scott got much better pitches to hit than he had in past seasons. As a result, he flourished, tying Reggie Jackson for the American League home run title with 36 and leading the league in RBI with 109. He also won his seventh straight Gold Glove.

By 1976, though, the magic had begun to fade. Jim Baumer had replaced Frank Lane (who had traded for Scott) as general manager and Alex Grammas had taken over for the fired Crandall. Scott struggled all season and Grammas eventually dropped him to seventh in the batting order, infuriating Boomer and allegedly causing him to say he was sick of playing in Milwaukee.

Scott denied having said that, but the die was cast. After the '77 season, Baumer dealt Scott and Bernie Carbo back to Boston for Cecil Cooper.

After Scott had departed, however, a new cast of special players were starting to make their presence felt, led by the irascible Gorman Thomas.

"Gorman was Gorman," Yount said. "He was a great, clutch, hard-nosed player that came to the ballpark for one reason and that was to play the game of baseball as hard and as tough as he could and do whatever he could to win the game."

"He was a great character, one of a kind," said former general manager Harry Dalton, who wangled a trade with Texas to get Thomas back for Bamberger in 1978. "He could be as exciting as anyone in the ballpark with a bat, or as frustrating. It was either feast or famine with Gorman."

Bamberger took the massive Thomas aside during spring training in 1978 and offered two pieces of advice: A home run counts the same whether it lands in the first row of bleachers or the last. So stop swinging so hard. Second, the center field job was his, so don't lose it.

Thomas was the glue that kept the Brewers clubhouse together. He would become the team leader in handing out nicknames and was responsible for two of the better ones — Mike Caldwell's "Mr. Warmth" and Jim Gantner's "Gumby."

"You know, from that cartoon 'Gumby and Pokey,'" Gantner said. "Gorman said I walked like Gumby, whatever that meant." But the name stuck and the rest, as they say, is history. "He was good at making up names," Gantner conceded.

Thomas also had his strange habits. On certain days, when he didn't feel like dealing with anyone, he would climb on top of the lockers and take a nap.

From the time he started playing every day in 1978 to the time he was traded in 1983, Thomas never hit higher than .259. He also led the league twice in strikeouts with 175 in 1979 and 170 more in 1980. But when he connected, he was a sight to behold.

In 1979, he led the American League in home runs with 45 and drove in 123 runs. He tied for the league lead in homers in 1982, pounding out 39 and knocking in 112. And from 1978–1982, he averaged 35 homers and 98 RBI. He also led the league in leaving pieces of his body on the turf while playing center field.

"One of the most aggressive center fielders I've ever seen," Bamberger said. "He went after everything."

Thomas was not the most agile of players and he always sported something on his face — be it a shaggy beard or a mustache. He looked anything like a protypical centerfielder but he always got the job done. And the city loved him. Absolutely loved him. He

Two close friends, Rollie Fingers and Pete Vuckovich, who also happened to win back-to-back Cy Young Awards in 1981 and 1982.

Manager Harvey Kuenn was never a genius with strategy, but he always seemed to know what worked. Part of what worked was always to throw Pete Vuckovich (right) every few days.

was one of them. He didn't look the part and that's what endeared him to Milwaukee. He was known to tip a few too many, known to speak his mind, known to live on the edge just a little. He did nothing half measure — all things that made Milwaukee love him even more.

That's why Brewers fans were stunned in 1983 when Dalton traded Thomas and pitcher Jamie Easterly to Cleveland for Rick Waits and Rick Manning.

Three years later, though, the Brewers re-signed Thomas and the city rejoiced. In an unscientific poll conducted by the *Milwaukee Journal*, a staggering 83 percent of fans said they were happy to see Thomas back. A sampling of positive comments included:

"The Brewers are so boring, they need something to liven them up."

"He's part of Milwaukee's folklore. A living legend."

"He's a typical Milwaukeean: A beer-drinking home-run hitter."

"We need a hero with the guts to swing for the bleachers in the ninth inning, both in the ballpark and in life. Gorman is that hero."

And 10 games after returning, Thomas rewarded those faithful followers by blasting a home run around the left field foul pole to beat the White Sox in 11 innings.

"To be honest, I just didn't want to strike out," said Thomas, who'd struck out twice earlier in the game. "I was the only person in the ballpark that knew it was a home run at first. With the shadows, the ball was hard to see. I just said: 'Don't hook.' I wasn't going to jump up and down, but it's a win and that's what counts."

That would be one of Gorman Thomas' last hurrahs for the Brewers, but he left a legacy that Brewers fans still talk about today.

"He was the embodiment of Milwaukee," former teammate Sal Bando said.

There was no talking about Gorman Thomas without mentioning his two soulmates from that era — pitchers Caldwell and Pete Vuckovich. Irreverant, crude, fun, mean-tempered, they also helped form the Milwaukee Brewers of the early '80s.

Caldwell especially meant a lot to the Brewers and the Brewers meant a lot to him.

"Obviously, they were the best years of my professional career," he said. "I have very fond memories of my years in Milwaukee."

Caldwell hadn't done a whole lot in his previous six years in the big leagues as chronic arm problems forced him to bounce from San Diego to San Francisco to Cincinnati before being traded to the Brewers for two minor leaguers.

But in his first full season with the Brewers in 1978, Caldwell blossomed under the tutelage of manager Bamberger, an ex-pitching coach with the Baltimore Orioles. Caldwell went 22–9 with a 2.37 ERA and a league best 23 complete games. He won 16 games the next season and 13 the following year, establishing himself as one of the league's best lefthanders.

Caldwell was no bargain to deal with on game days.

"I guess I got a little sharp with people on the days I was pitching," he said of that apparently derogatory nickname. "If someone asked me a question, I gave them an honest answer."

ALL STAR GAME 1975

WORLD SERIES '82

One victory away from ecstasy

Brewer defense makes Caldwell lucky winner

A long list of heroes from Sunday's victory

SportsWeekend

A grand, grand, grand hit

A special 3-way hug

Selig's tears tell a story

Coaches take a hard line on NFL scouts

They called Jim Slaton "Pops." But no one was happier than the veteran right-hander when the Brewers reached the World Series in 1982. After years of playing for bad ballclubs, it was the culmination of his stellar career.

"He was a gruff and dirty-looking kind of guy," Bando said. "Things didn't come easily to him but he always battled."

In the 1982 World Series, Caldwell was at his best. He won twice, pitched 17⅔ innings and although he gave up 19 hits (14 in one game), he only allowed four runs.

"That was the highlight for me," said Caldwell, who is still the club's all-time leader in complete games (81) and second in wins (102) and shutouts (18). "I was very appreciative of baseball in Milwaukee. If I had a chance to get to the big leagues as a coach, Milwaukee is the place I'd like to go."

Vuckovich was the right-handed equivalent of Caldwell. Imposing with his dark glare and bushy mustache, Vuke never backed down from a challenge on or off the mound.

In one of the guttiest pitching performances in Brewers history, Vuckovich dragged himself off a sick bed to pitch Game Four of the 1981 playoffs against the Yankees. Wracked by the flu, Vuckovich threw up between innings and even occasionally while on the mound, but still managed to throw a five-hitter at the Yankees and win 2–1 to even the series.

Vuckovich never lost sight of what the game was about. In a late-season game in '81, the Brewers were battling the Red Sox with both teams still in the title hunt. Boston's Jerry Remy doubled off Vuckovich and when he stopped at second, Vuckovich was staring at him. Suddenly Vuke stuck out his tongue at Remy and returned to the mound. Remy was stunned.

"Did he do what I think he did?" Remy asked umpire Jim Evans. Evans smiled and nodded.

Vuckovich said afterward: "You've got to have a little fun out there."

Vuckovich won 14 games that first season in '81 and came back

161

to win the Cy Young Award in 1982, posting an 18–6 record and a 3.34 ERA.

Vuckovich, Caldwell and Thomas were also considered the fathers of a game that made the Brewers famous in those days — the infamous flip game. Today's Brewers still play it, but it doesn't even compare to the war waged by that '82 team. The consensus was that if a flip game didn't result in a fistfight, it wasn't a good game. It was relaxation, it was fun and it served to bond the team together. Even prior to the seventh game of the World Series, the Brewers played flip. The routine never altered.

Insults flew (though no one could make fun of Don Money's rather prominent ears or Thomas' penchant for striking out) along with the ball, as players flipped the ball to teammates as hard as possible. Naturally, if injuries didn't result, it wasn't considered a really good game either.

"It got a little rough," Caldwell said. "I remember (Jim) Gantner got a black eye and a tooth knocked out. Bando had his foot stepped on. Things like that. I don't think they're allowed to play it anymore. You can't afford to have a $3 million player doing that."

And there were more heroes.

Perhaps no pitcher is more identified with the Brewers than right-hander Jim Slaton, nicknamed "Pops" by, who else, Gorman Thomas. He spent all but one of his big league seasons with the Brewers after being called up in 1971. Slaton saw all the bad times and was thankful to have stayed around long enough to see the good. He was the winner of Game Four in the 1982 World Series.

"I saw a lot of faces come through this organization, so getting to the World Series was so special to me," Slaton said.

From 1973 through 1979 (including one season in Detroit), Slaton won at least 11 games and never had an ERA higher than 4.50. It was the kind of consistency a new Brewers team needed but rarely took advantage of. Though he retired after the 1983 season, Slaton remains the Brewers all-time leader in games started (268), wins (117), shutouts (19) and innings pitched.

One player who didn't spend many seasons in Milwaukee but had a huge impact was baseball's consummate relief pitcher, Rollie Fingers. He pitched only four years with the Brewers, but his contributions were immense. That's why Fingers' No. 34 is one of only two numbers retired by the club (Hank Aaron's is the other).

Fingers was part of what Brewers fans still call "The Trade," a deal that brought Rollie, Vuckovich and catcher Ted Simmons to Milwaukee from St. Louis in 1981 and opened the door for the Brewers' ascension to the top of the American League.

Fingers' performance in 1981 alone has been called the greatest season a relief pitcher could have. He won six games, saved 28 others in the strike-abbreviated season and posted an earned run average of 1.04. And at crunch time, Fingers was even better. Fingers was involved in 12 of the Brewers' final 15 victories.

Big Rollie was on the same kind of pace in '82 when he tore an elbow muscle while pitching on September 2. The injury forced him out for rest of that season — not to mention the playoffs and the World Series. Check through those Series losses to the Cardinals and you'll probably conclude, as Brewers fans do, that Fingers would have made the winning difference.

"That was probably my low point," Fingers said. "All the way up to August was great, and then I tore that muscle. I tried everything to get back that year but I couldn't."

Major surgery followed and Fingers missed the entire 1983 season recuperating. But amazingly, he was back in '84.

"I'm a little surprised at the way I've thrown," he said then. "I didn't think I'd be able to pitch in as many ball games and as many innings as I have. I thought I'd get in two, maybe three, games a week. But it's been more like four or five games a week. I may not be throwing as hard as I used to, but I'm getting guys out. I think experience has probably helped me out quite a bit."

In 1984, Fingers appeared in 33 games and saved 23 for the Brewers before a herniated disc in his back closed him down for the season. He fought back again in '85, saving 17 more before finally retiring at the end of the year.

Yes, his career was punctuated by injury, and perhaps he wasn't the reliever he was in his epic years in Oakland, but Rollie Fingers helped bring the Brewers to that next level and he'll always be remembered for it.

Just the opposite was Money, who toiled for the Brewers for 11 years. He played in the awful times in the early '70s. He played in the glorious times in the early

'80s. And he played in between. Along the way, Money earned a reputation as a superb gloveman at third base and elsewhere, a clutch hitter and class individual.

But time moves on and in January 1984, the Brewers released Money, who went on to play in Japan.

"I was with the Brewers in thick and thin," he said at the time. "I more or less grew up with the club and the players. You just realize you won't be seeing the guys everyday anymore and I'll miss that. You know it had to end sometime. I just wish I could've finished my career in Milwaukee. Well, I guess I did."

Never a flashy, overt type, Money toiled in quiet efficiency. He was a four-time All-Star and set an American League record in 1974 with most errorless chances at third with 257. That same season, he set league records for highest fielding percentage (.989), fewest errors in a season (five), most consecutive errorless games (88) and most consecutive errorless games in a season (86).

Money's strength was his versatility, as he played every infield position as well as left field during his career. But he also finished in the top five all-time in Brewers history in several offensive categories — including runs, hits, doubles, singles, walks and at-bats.

"Overall, I guess I'd have to rate my career as nothing outstanding, but very steady," Money said. "I always prided myself on defense. From 1970 to 1977, I'd have to say I was as good as any third baseman in either league. I was happy I was able to play as long as I did. The fans of

It became a habit for Dan Plesac to come to the Brewers rescue. He holds the club record for all-time saves and saves in a season.

Rollie Fingers became the second Brewers player to have his number retired. Hank Aaron was the other.

Milwaukee and Wisconsin always treated me great from the time I got there. They never got on me and they are always supportive of me. I apreciated that."

Which brings to mind two players who perhaps weren't appreciated as much as they probably should've been. But then Dan Plesac and Rob Deer were in high profile positions in which failure was terribly magnified.

Plesac burst on the scene in 1987 as baseball's next great young reliever. During that wild season, the left-handed Plesac saved five of the games in Milwaukee's memorable 13–0 start. He had 18 saves at the break and was Milwaukee's only representative in the All-Star game. An elbow injury in August cut down his effectiveness and he posted only five more saves, but those 23 were still fourth-best in the league.

"Because of the great start I had, people have sort of come to expect and demand a lot and I demand that of myself," Plesac said of his explosion onto the scene. "Short work to me is a lot like hitting — you have good streaks and you have bad streaks. You can't get too up when you're hot and you can't get down on yourself when you're struggling. There are a lot of things you just can't control, but I feel every time I go out there I'm capable of doing a good job."

Plesac kept that up in 1988, registering another 30 saves, a 2.41 earned run average and a second straight trip to the All-Star game. And in 1989, he was even better, recording a team-record 33 saves, setting a club all-time saves record (breaking Fingers'

record of 97), posting a 2.35 ERA and being selected for yet another All-Star game.

But in 1990, hitters began to figure out Plesac and his effectiveness diminished, even though he still picked up 24 saves, had a 69 percent success rate and ranked among league leaders in appearances, saves and games finished. In 1991, he started in the bullpen but was eventually moved to the starting rotation — where he finished 2–7 with a 4.29 ERA. By '92, he became a set-up man out of the bullpen, ironically posting his first winning record since his rookie season in 1986 and his lowest ERA since 1989.

Following the '92 season, he signed a free-agent contract with the Chicago Cubs, but Plesac left Milwaukee with team records in saves (133) and games (365) and was fifth all-time in ERA (3.21).

While Plesac was under the microscope as a closer, Deer's particular job was that of power hitter. He came to Milwaukee in 1986 as part of a trade with San Francisco. And though it was a great opportunity for Deer, who'd been nothing more than a part-time player with the Giants, he also knew nothing was guaranteed with the Brewers.

Deer went to spring training 1986 as a non-roster player and impressed the Brewers enough to earn a spot on the big club. In the season opener in Chicago, Deer showed just what he was capable of doing as he took a pitch from future Hall of Famer Tom Seaver and knocked it out of Comiskey Park — clear out onto 34th Street.

"I didn't want to leave any doubts about the opportunity," said Deer, who had spent nearly seven full seasons in the minors before getting that opportunity. "I worked hard for it and I didn't want it to slip away."

It didn't. Deer went on to hit 33 home runs that season, the most by a Brewers player since Gorman Thomas in 1982 and the most ever by a Brewers right fielder. Deer's 11 homers in August missed by one the record set by Thomas in 1979. He also became the first Brewers player to hit 20 or more homers in five consecutive seasons. And, as power hitters will do, Deer also struck out 179 times.

"Sure, he's going to strike out," manager Tom Trebelhorn said, "but he's also going to hit the ball a long way and that's important to the club. He was given a chance here and he took full advantage of it. He has that hunger for the game because his approach to the game is always 100 percent."

Over the next four years, Deer averaged 26 home runs, 74 runs batted in and 161 strikeouts — alternately bringing cheers and boos from the County Stadium faithful. But he always made things interesting.

Deer left the Brewers after the 1990 season, signing as a free agent with the Detroit Tigers.

Then there is the enigma that was Cecil Cooper.

If anyone could play a quiet 11 seasons in one city, it was Cooper. The bespectacled first baseman never courted media attention, never did anything outrageous, never sought the spotlight. As a result, many Brewers fans simply took him for granted — which was probably a mistake.

"A great, great ballplayer," former manager Bamberger said.

"We had a lot of great ballplayers and he (Cooper) kind of got lost in the shuffle. If he had wanted to, there's no doubt in my mind he could've hit 35 to 40 homers a season. But he knew that wasn't his job. He was probably one of the best hitters I've ever seen."

And, perhaps more than anything, that's how Cooper should be remembered.

"He was just a pure hitter," Yount said. "He hit the ball to all fields, he hit for a high average and had a lot of power to go with it. He was a great player."

From the time he came to Milwaukee in 1977 as part of trade with Boston that sent Scott and Bernie Carbo back to the Red Sox, the left-handed hitting Cooper was one of those players that a manager could pencil in and forget about. He was an eight-time .300 hitter and a marvelous first baseman. And while Yount, Molitor and Gantner have grabbed most of the ink for longevity and consistency, Cooper has to rank right up there.

Cooper hit .300 or better every season from 1977 through 1983, drove in 100 runs four times and nailed 20 or more homers five times. But his best season was 1980, when he hit .352, belted 25 homers and led the American League with 122 RBI.

Cooper retired after the 1987 season and took his place among the top five Brewers all-time in just about every offensive category. In fact, he finished exactly one point (.303 to .302) behind Molitor as Milwaukee's all-time leading hitter.

Coop's career ended rather unceremoniously, as he rode the bench through the second half of

Rob Deer is the only Brewers player ever to hit 20 home runs in five consecutive seasons.

When Cecil Cooper's career ended at the end of the 1987 season, he didn't want any fuss to be made about it. In his last post-game meal, Coop sat quietly by his locker, ate his dinner and left. And that was that.

the '87 season. There was no Cecil Cooper Appreciation Day because, unfortunately, that's the way his career had gone.

In 1985, a 27-year-old rookie left-hander erupted onto the scene for the Milwaukee Brewers. And for four seasons, Teddy Higuera staked his claim as one of the best pitchers in baseball. In one particular game during his first season, Higuera went into the baseball cathedral known as Yankee Stadium, fired a five-hitter and beat the red-hot Yanks 1–0, giving him his 15th win and setting a record for wins by a Brewers rookie. That performance even staggered Bamberger.

"He's pitched so many good games," Bambi said. "But this one — 1–0 in Yankee Stadium — I'd have to say was the best. It was a fantastic game."

Such performances became almost routine for Higuera. In 1986, he was 20–11 with a 2.79 ERA and 207 strikeouts and finished second to Boston's Roger Clemens for the Cy Young Award. Over the next four years, Higuera won 54 more games. In 1987, he set a club record with 32 straight scoreless innings and missed a no-hitter against Kansas City by four outs.

"He's the kind of pitcher who says, 'I've got a lead and three innings to go. I'm going to finish this game off myself,'" Bamberger said. "That's the way (Catfish) Hunter, (Jim) Palmer, (Dave) McNally and (Mike) Cuellar were. Guys who struggle early, then get by those first three innings and then get better and better."

But in 1991, injuries began to plague Higuera. He tore his rotator cuff in spring training and

pitched only 36 big-league innings. In '92, he had more rotator cuff surgery and missed the entire season, pitching only 19 innings in the minors. By 1993, Higuera seemed ready to come back, but a shoulder problem — followed by a sprained ankle — sidelined him again. Finally, by August 1993, Higuera did return to the rotation.

So who were the best of the Brewers' best?

If you were going to put together a silver anniversary Milwaukee Brewers team, who would be on it? That question was posed to a lot of people who have watched the Brewers over the years. Put together an all-star Brewers team and see what kind of arguments it might cause. Some of the choices were obvious no-brainers, but some others, ah, you'll have to decide for yourself.

Designated Hitter: An easy pick, Paul Molitor. He may have played eight positions (including DH) during his career and excelled at all of them, but he was a hitter pure and simple.

First base: No-brainer number two, Cecil Cooper.

Second base: Who else but Jim Gantner?

Shortstop: Are you kidding? Robin Yount.

Third base: A tough choice, but it's Don Money for sheer longevity and overall consistency.

Left field: Ben Oglivie, if only for that sliding catch against the Orioles in the 1982 finale.

Center field: Gorman Thomas, mostly because he was Gorman but also because even the magnificent Yount can't play two positions at once.

Right field: A great case can be made for Charlie Moore or Sixto

Lezcano, but the consensus went modern and took current standout Darryl Hamilton, a star in the making.

Catcher: Ted Simmons, with apologies to B.J. Surhoff.

Relief pitcher: Rollie Fingers or Dan Plesac? Is that a tough choice? Not really. The man with the handlebar mustache was the best ever.

Right-handed starter: Pete Vuckovich won a Cy Young award but Jim Slaton is Milwaukee's all-time leading winner. Hmmm. The jury was nearly deadlocked but Slaton got the nod.

Left-handed pitcher: Teddy Higuera or Mike Caldwell? Nobody could sort out that one. Pick your favorite.

Look back over that entire group now, and something becomes pretty obvious. Even for a quasi-expansion team, the Brewers wound up running an awful lot of talent out onto that County Stadium turf.

As you may have noticed, a lot of those players come from those powerful teams of the late '70s and early '80s, teams consisting of players who needed long leashes and little motivation.

Tom Trebelhorn was perhaps the most organized manager in Brewers history. He knew the game backward and forward and he infused the Brewers with the kind of enthusiasm that usually doesn't work in the Major Leagues.

One manager was perfect for dealing with them as they adjusted to the early stages of success, the irrepresible Bamberger. In deference to Dave Bristol, Del Crandall and Alex Grammas who preceeded him, Bamberger was the first Brewers manager to give the job a tinge of color. He was funny, fun-loving and he knew his baseball.

"George took over the city," said the man who hired him, general manager Harry Dalton. "He was just right for Milwaukee."

Bamberger roared into town in 1978 and, along with Dalton, made the kind of wide-sweeping changes that turned the Brewers into contenders for the next five years. Had his health not slipped, he probably would've been around for that 1981 playoff appearance as well as the World Series in '82. He was a combination of free spirit, grandfather and baseball guru, a guy a lot like his eventual successor, Harvey Kuenn.

"Bambi was just a fun-loving guy," said Robin Yount. "And he knew his baseball."

He is best known for helping the Brewers improve an incredible 26 games in the win column between 1977 and 1978. In 1979, they were even better, winning 95 games and finishing second in the AL East behind the Orioles.

He is also the guy who reputedly taught pitcher Mike Caldwell how to throw the "Staten Island sinker," what some might call a spitball. He also, after watching a triple play against his club, uttered the famous line, "That triple play took us right out of the inning."

But what he really brought was a sense of how to win, a quality distinctly lacking in the Brewers organization. How far the Brewers could have gone under Bamberger won't be known because of his 1980 heart attack that eventually forced him to retire.

He was back in 1982 as manager of the disastrous New York Mets. He never had a chance. The Mets lost 97 games in Bambi's first year and were 16–30 in 1983 when he was fired. Meanwhile, the Brewers had fallen on equally hard times. Under first-year manager Rene Lachemann in 1984, the Brewers collapsed, falling to 67–94, snapping a streak of seven straight winning seasons. Lachemann barely made it out of that season before being fired.

Bamberger, architect of the first Brewers dynasty, was unemployed and the Brewers, adrift again, needed a boss. The fit seemed perfect. So Bamberger was re-hired for 1985 to revive the franchise he'd brought to life originally.

"If it wasn't Milwaukee, I wouldn't be back," Bamberger said. "I was treated great by Bud Selig, Harry Dalton, the organization, the media and the fans. When you get treated like I was treated and you leave, you always have that feeling that you'd like to come back. I'm going to try and get the maximum out of every player's ability. If we can get everyone to play to their potential, we'll be all right. That's what I'm being hired for. We'll probably make some changes along the way."

But it wasn't that easy and Bamberger could feel it. He was finding out that you can't relive the past.

"The first time everything was so positive all the way through the organization," said Bamberger. "The second time, it was more negative. Everything was at a standstill. Players should have been moved that weren't moved."

Even Bamberger couldn't help this time. In 1985, the Brewers won only four more games than the year before and they were sputtering again in 1986 when Bamberger retired September 26.

To finish out the season, the Brewers tabbed third base coach Tom Trebelhorn, an ex-school teacher who wasn't even supposed to be coaching with the big club. Treb was supposed to spend the '86 season as minor league hitting coach and manager for the Brewers' Rookie League team in Helena, Montana. But a bizarre twist put Trebelhorn on the fast track he never expected. A gas explosion at the Brewers' new spring training facility in Chandler, Arizona, seriously injured Tony Muser, who was to begin his second year as Bamberger's third base coach. With Muser out, Trebelhorn was promoted.

Milwaukee loved George Bamberger and Bamberger loved Milwaukee. Here, Bambi and his wife, Wilma, salute the County Stadium crowd.

Six months later, Trebelhorn was managing a major league team and on October 1, he was officially named the Brewers manager. It was a glorious triumph for one of the organization's truly nice guys.

"I still remember the night Treb was hired," said Tom Skibosh, the Brewer director of media realtions. "Here was a good guy who did his homework, who had paid his dues. I was really happy for him. The two of us walked out to the parking lot here at the stadium and we hugged. Two guys in our parking lot, hugging."

Trebelhorn brought a different style to the Brewers. Whereas Bamberger was more of a fly-by-the-seat-of-his-pants type, Trebelhorn was a stickler for order and organization.

"He was a very intelligent manager, he studied the game," Yount said. "He knew the ins and outs, knew every number about every player. He had as much enthusiasm and as much hard work as any manager that I played for. He was a positive thinker and just a real, fiery gung-ho type guy."

And that attitude carried over into that improbable 1987 season, where the Brewers won 13 straight right out of the gate and 17 of their first 18. The momentum finally came to a halt, though, as they then went on a club-record 12-game losing streak. But Treb had instilled his beliefs. His teams were going to play smart, they were going to run and they were going to know what they were doing every second they were on the field.

"He was the most organized manager I've ever played for," said B.J. Surhoff, whom Trebelhorn installed as starting catcher

barely two months into his rookie season.

Treb led the Brewers to a 91–71 mark that season and followed it up with an 87–75 performance in 1988, tied for third in AL East but only two games out of first place. The Brewers slipped the next two years, to 81–81 in 1989 and 74–88 in 1990.

And, as it is in most professional sports, when a couple of down years are strung together, the questions begin to arise, the uncertainty grows. So it happened with Trebelhorn in 1991. The Brewers got off to another slow start and by August 3 were mired at 43–60, 15 games out of first place. But something strange happened. From that point, the Brewers turned it around, got some superb pitching, timely hitting and went on a tear the rest of the season. And though they never really made a run at the AL East title, they finished as baseball's hottest team, winning 40 of their final 59 games to notch an 83–79 record.

But by that stage, it was too late for Treb. The Brewers, in the kind of sweeping changes that hadn't been seen since the mid-1970s, cleaned house as Dalton was reassigned, replaced as general manager by Sal Bando, and Trebelhorn was fired and replaced by Phil Garner, a long-time player who was most recently third base coach for the Houston Astros.

The future had begun. One more time. ❖

No.	PLAYERS	Pos	1	2	3	4	5	6	7
38	GERHART	LF	6-3		W2 (BB)			K5	
17	BURLESON	2B	K1		K3			8	
8	RIPKEN	SS	8			L-5		9	
33	MURRAY	1B		7		2F		6-4 / 4 (BB) DP	
19	LYNN	CF		8		8		4-3	
25	KNIGHT	3B		W1 (BB)		7		6	
27	LACY	DH	L-7				W3 (BB)		
37	SHELBY	RF			K2	K4			
6	RAYFORD	C			6	L-5			
	Sub.								
	SUMMARY		0	0	0	0	0	0	0

PITCHING	WLS	RCD.	IP	H	R	ER	BB	SO	HR	WP	HB	BK
NIEVES	W	2-0	9	0	0	0	5	7				

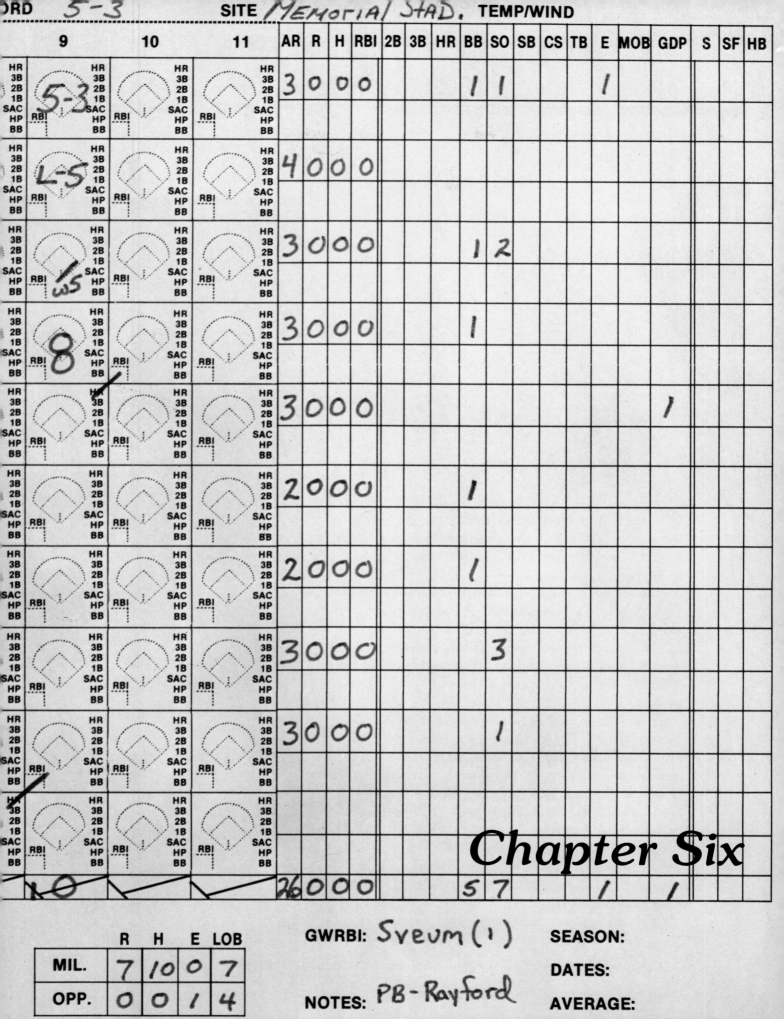

RD 5-3 SITE MEMORIAL STAD. TEMP/WIND

9	10	11	AR	R	H	RBI	2B	3B	HR	BB	SO	SB	CS	TB	E	MOB	GDP	S	SF	HB
5-3			3	0	0	0				1	1				1					
L-5			4	0	0	0														
4-3			3	0	0	0				1	2									
8			3	0	0	0				1										
			3	0	0	0											1			
			2	0	0	0				1										
			2	0	0	0				1										
			3	0	0	0					3									
			3	0	0	0				1										
10			26	0	0	0				5	7				1		1			

	R	H	E	LOB
MIL.	7	10	0	7
OPP.	0	0	1	4

GWRBI: Sveum (1) SEASON:

NOTES: PB - Rayford DATES:

AVERAGE:

Chapter Six

It's Been Fun

SOMETIMES, YOU JUST HAVE TO SIT BACK and enjoy it all. Don't look for a reason, don't look for an answer, don't look for any grand, underlying logic.

Just smile, shake your head in wonder and say, "Well, that's baseball." Baseball in Milwaukee.

The Brewers have made a few entries of their own in that dizzying diary of this game that no one has yet to figure out after well over a century.

Can anyone, for example, explain 1987's "Team Streak"? Doubtful, very doubtful. Can anyone explain some of the great one-year, one-game wonders in Brewers history? Guys like Bobby Coluccio, Bill Parsons, Pedro Garcia, Danny Walton, Mark Brouhard, Dale Sveum? Again, very doubtful.

Can anyone explain why Whitey Herzog was furious during a trip to County Stadium? Of course not. Then again, that's baseball. Just sit back and enjoy it.

Perhaps nothing in Brewers history defied

Fun-loving Rick Manning never did catch a break with Brewers fans. They railed against him first because he was part of a trade that sent the beloved Gorman Thomas away. Fans had further reason to get on him when he delivered the game-winning hit that denied Paul Molitor a chance to keep his 39-game hitting streak alive.

explanation more than that bizarre, wondrous, perplexing 1987 team, dubbed "Team Streak" for what would become obvious reasons.

That club took fans on a precipitous six-month journey that finally ended with the Brewers finishing third in the AL East with a solid 91–71 record. But that record tells none of the story of what may have been the wildest season the Brewers have experienced so far. Or ever might again.

Nothing in spring training indicated what was in store for the Brewers that season. They had a new, untried manager in Tom Trebelhorn, a ex-school teacher with the kind of boyish enthusiasm that usually doesn't work in the cynical big leagues.

In fact, in a preseason *Milwaukee Journal* poll, 74 pecent of those responding couldn't even name the Brewers manager. Those Brewers had a young, untested pitching staff featuring five starters with a combined four years of major league experience and the entire roster featured 14 players with one year or less in the bigs.

So no one, least of all the rational Milwaukee fan, was expecting much of anything when the Brewers opened the 1987 campaign on a bright, glorious April afternoon against the defending league champion Boston Red Sox. But 52,585 patrons decided to show up, anyway — perhaps mostly out of curiousity.

Paul Molitor, in a prophetic stroke, opened the Brewers' season with a triple and was knocked home immediately by Robin Yount. Something wonderful had begun and no one yet knew it.

The Brewers won that one behind a fireballing young Mexican named Teddy Higuera and then won two more as rookie Billy Jo Robidoux knocked in a game-winning run and Rob Deer belted two three-run homers and another rookie, B.J. Surhoff, hit an eighth-inning homer to beat the Red Sox 12–11.

"The veterans are playing with the enthusiasm of rookies and the rookies are playing with the poise of veterans," general manager Harry Dalton said.

The Brewers then hit the road for three games in Texas. Eight-run innings in the first two games keyed victories and Surhoff's two-run single in the 12th made it 6–0 to start the season.

This, figured Brewers fans, was worth paying attention to.

From there, the Brewers headed to their perennial snake pit, Baltimore's Memorial Stadium. They won the first two against the Orioles with sheer power. Deer and Greg Brock banged out three hits in the first game and Molitor, Deer, Brock, Jim Gantner and Yount smacked home runs to power the next one.

Then came April 15, a drizzly, uncomfortable night in Baltimore, the night America finally stood up and took notice of the Milwaukee Brewers.

On center stage that particular evening was a 22-year-old Puerto Rican, left-hander Juan Nieves, who was already in his third season with the big club and on the verge on stardom.

Things started innocently enough as Nieves retired the Orioles in order in the first inning. In the second, rookie left fielder Jim Paciorek, starting in place of

Row 5: L-R Greg Brock, Rob Deer, Chris Bosio, Dan Plesac, Bill Wegman, Mark Clear, Len Barker, Jim Paciorek and Glenn Braggs.

Row 4: L-R Paul Molitor, Rick Manning, Mike Birkbeck, John Henry Johnson, Bill Schroeder, Dale Sveum, Juan Nieves, Cecil Cooper, Robin Yount and B.J. Surhoff.

Row 3: L-R Assistant Home Clubhouse Attendant George Spelius, Trainer John Adam, Mike Felder, Teddy Higuera, Chuck Crim, Jim Gantner, Juan Castillo, Visiting Clubhouse Manager Jim Ksicinski and Traveling Secretary Jimmy Bank.

Row 2: L-R Equipment Manager Tony Migliaccio, Coaches Chuck Hartenstein, Andy Etchebarren, Manager Tom Trebelhorn, Coaches Larry Haney, Tony Muser and Dave Hilton.

Row 1: L-R Bat Boys: Joe Gessay, Charley Weber, Con Geary, David Richter and Steve Sampson.

The 1987 Milwaukee Brewers, who will now and forever be known as "Team Streak."

Deer, made a sliding catch on the dangerous Eddie Murray. Nice play, sure, but so what?

Meanwhile, Nieves wasn't exactly feeling like a world beater on the mound. "I was really uncomfortable out there," he said. "My stuff was awful. I felt bad. I couldn't throw a slider. My changeup was up. I felt like a pregnant lady. But eventually everything came together. I just kept throwing and all of a sudden, everything just turned around."

For six innings, Nieves dueled with Baltimore veteran Mike Flanagan and the Brewers held a slim 1–0 lead, thanks to a solo homer by another rookie, Dale Sveum. It was for that reason

that, despite the fact that a no-hitter was in progress, Trebelhorn thought about pulling Nieves in favor of a fresh reliever.

"It's a great achievement, but then so are the next 12 years in the big leagues," Trebelhorn said. "You have to do what's right."

He did. He left Nieves on the mound.

Pitching coach Chuck Hartenstein did make one visit to chat with the wonderkid, after Nieves walked Murray on four pitches to open the seventh.

"When I looked in his eyes, I did not see a problem," Hartenstein said. "I saw somebody who was in control of everything."

The Brewers broke the game

open in the seventh inning, scoring three times. They added three more in the eighth on a Brock homer and one more in the ninth on a Glenn Braggs blast. With the outcome decided, the 11,407 fans on hand wanted to see some history.

In the bottom of the ninth, the previously hostile crowd stood for Nieves.

"It's not my ballpark," he said. "When you pitch in somebody else's park, you don't pay attention to fans."

Nieves knew that if the no-hitter was going to end, the Oriole hitters who could do it were coming up that inning. Ken Gerhart led off and grounded out easily to Molitor at third. Veteran Rick Burleson was next and he lined out to Molitor. The next hitter, future Hall of Famer Cal Ripken, walked on four pitches that weren't even close to the strike zone.

And up stepped the formidable Murray, who turned on a fastball that Nieves had left high in the strike zone and sent it into the gap in right center.

"Off the bat, I thought it was going to hang a little," Trebelhorn said. "Then it started to fall and I thought: Here's the kid's no-hitter and shutout as well."

Not quite.

Yount, only in his second full season as a centerfielder, galloped after the liner and made the grab with an all-out, parallel-to-the-ground dive — a spectacular play that preserved the first no-hitter in Brewers history.

"I saw it all the way," said Yount. "I felt like I got a decent jump on it. I chased it and it fell in my glove. Games like this, you get pretty excited. Those things don't happen very often. You don't get too many chances to take part in it. I was going to give it every effort not to fall in."

Catcher Bill Schroeder also thought Nieves had lost his no-hitter. "But Robin just kept gaining ground on it," he said.

Murray, though, had another opinion. "It had no chance at all," he sniffed.

Nieves had not only pitched the first-ever Brewers no-hitter, he'd dramatically helped the Brewers move to a giddy 9–0 start. He walked five, struck out seven (all swinging) and did not allow a runner past first base.

"All I know is I'm damned proud to be part of it," Schroeder said. "I'm proud of Juan. He showed me a lot. All the credit goes to the left-hander. The way he pitched, Bingo Long and the guy with the monkey could have called that game."

After that historic night in Baltimore, even the Brewers were beginning to believe something magical was happening.

"People probably think this is a joke, but it's not," Nieves said. "It's a taste of what's to come the rest of the way. We're back. No mercy."

For Nieves, sadly, the no-hitter would prove to be the pinnacle of his brief, star-crossed career. He would go on to win 14 games that season and throw nearly 200 innings. But things only went downhill from there.

Nieves was plagued with shoulder problems throughout the 1988 season, though he did manage to win seven games and even picked up his first save. But the following year, just before his

Chapter Seven

Deep, Deep Center

OCTOBER 30, 1991, THE MILWAUKEE BREWERS took a gamble.

This was a huge gamble. In fact, one of the biggest the franchise had taken in years. Popular Tom Trebelhorn had just been fired as manager and the Brewers knew they needed a replacement who could mold talent and organize players the way Treb had done.

There were plenty of candidates, as is always the case when a big league managing job comes open. There were dozens of guys who knew baseball, who knew players and who knew how to manage and the Brewers seemingly could take their pick.

But the Brewers, who have rarely followed the mainstream, chose to ignore the conventional wisdom that said they should select a manager with years of experience, if not necessarily years of success.

The Brewers knew something about a third base coach with the Houston Astros, an ex-player with absolutely no managing experience but with a feel for the game that few had.

Sal Bando was named the Brewers general manager in 1991.

This was Phil Garner, known in some circles by the tough-guy nickname of "Scrap Iron." Garner had played 16 big league seasons with five different teams. He'd been to All-Star games and he'd been to the World Series. He'd also known the pain of being released by a club, of being traded, of being told he just didn't have what it took anymore.

In short, Garner knew success and failure as a player, a commodity that cannot be taught.

"I wasn't sure if the Brewers were serious at first when they interviewed me for the job," Garner said.

They were. Very. In the end, despite no managing experience and barely two years as a coach, Garner was hired to take the Brewers forward. Raised eyebrows could be seen everywhere in baseball.

"The type of person Phil is, with his work ethic and his personality, we feel we made the right choice for this organization to take it to the next level," said General Manager Sal Bando, who had just recently been elevated to that post himself as Harry Dalton became Bud Selig's special assistant. "Phil is a very open person, aggressive, yet someone the players can relate to. His demeanor in itself was a better match for our club and where we want to go."

Yes, there were doubters, both inside Milwaukee and out. Who was this guy? And why pick him? Especially with so much managerial timber out there?

It was simple. Garner conveyed the scrappy, hard-nosed, never-give-up attitude that the Brewers needed. And what he lacked in managerial experience, the club's brain trust believed Garner could make up with his intricate knowledge of the game, his enthusiasm and his willingness to keep plugging.

"A coach in the Pittsburgh Pirates organization first called me Scrap Iron," Garner said. "He said I could be bent and beat up but I always kept coming back. Just like an old piece of scrap iron. It just kind of stuck. I never really minded the name but it's not like I go around calling myself that."

The name fits, though. And soon enough, Garner's attitude rubbed off on his new baseball team. All those initial smirks turned to nods of respect and maybe a little amazement in 1992 — after all, the Brewers roared through another unlikely season for a franchise that has had its share of them.

"My basic philosophy is to take a look at what you have on the field, try to match it up the best you can with game situations and find out which players you think are going to fit those situations best," Garner said. "I think all managers would like to have about six guys that hit 20 homers, or maybe four or five guys who run like world-class sprinters. But you don't, so you have to look at the available talent pool and see how you can put it together to make it work."

Garner did an uncanny job of that in his first season. The Brewers did sputter early under their new skipper but, even while they hovered just under .500, there were hints that these guys were on to something new, something exciting.

Garner had his Brewers running. All the time. In any situation. In every game. His philosophy was to put pressure on the opposing defense, somewhat like an aggressive offensive coordinator in football. Force the defense to make a play and make them choose the right one.

This was a new approach for the Brewers and slowly it began to work.

By the All-Star break, the Brewers were 45–41, third in the AL East, 7½ games out of first place. Not bad for a first-year manager, a first-year staff and a team with several new players.

But the best was yet to come. The Brewers won 10 of their final 15 games in July and then in August, they went through a remarkable stretch during which they simply battered the first-place Blue Jays.

In seven games with the Jays, the Brewers won four, outscoring them 55–12 — including a 22–2 trouncing in Toronto. In that game, the Brewers set American League records with 31 hits and 22 singles and they tacked on three club records.

The Brewers made their run at the AL East title in September, notching a 20–7 record that month. In a home finale reminiscent of those electric days in the early 1980s, the Brewers beat the Oakland A's 5–3 on September 27, completing a three-game sweep and pulling the Brewers within 2½ games of Toronto with six to play.

It wasn't supposed to be like this, was it?

After that victory over Oakland, a standing-room only crowd of nearly 55,000 rose and saluted its overachieving bunch of Brewers, a team that had played over its head all season. The players responded by returning to the field and applauding their fans. It was just like the good old days.

"The players need to take a curtain call," Garner said. "They could not have played more inspiring ball than they have the last five or six homestands. There was an air of excitement all around today."

Bud Selig remembered that day, too. "It was one of the most exciting things I'd seen all year," he said. "It gave me chills."

With two wins to open October, Milwaukee closed within two games of the Blue Jays but the gallant charge ended the next day, when they lost in Oakland and were eliminated from the race.

The Brewers finished 92–70, four games out of first place, having posted the highest club victory total since 1982. They also earned a new respect around the league. Milwaukee led baseball in stolen bases with 256, the first time an AL East team had ever stolen more than 200 bases in a season. In all, six Brewers stole 15 or more bases. The Brewers also led the league in pitching and fielding and were second in hitting.

"We had a staff that worked extremely hard, that worked intelligently and that was always looking for an edge," Garner said. "We had an owner I felt comfortable with. If I made a mistake tonight, he wasn't going to call me up and say, 'What the hell were you doing?' I didn't have to second-guess myself based on him.

In seven seasons with the Brewers, right-hander Chris Bosio cut his name into the top 10 in just about every team pitching category including games started, complete games, wins, strikeouts and shutouts.

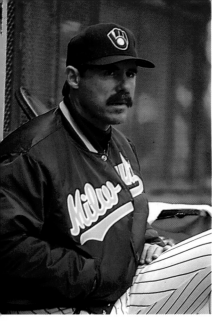

One of Bando's first duties was to hire Phil Garner as manager, replacing Tom Trebelhorn. Though he'd had no managing experience, Garner still led the Brewers to a stunning second-place finish in 1992.

(Opposite) It has become a Brewers tradition for the players to salute the crowd after the final home game of the season. A crowd of 55,000 was on hand for the 1992 finale, a 5–3 win over Oakland.

"I had a general manager who gave me 100 percent support. When some tough decisions had to be made, he didn't tell me which way to go. He told me to do what I needed to do and he'd back me."

It was a season that officially ushered in the new era of Milwaukee Brewers baseball. There was the new manager, who, despite his Herculean efforts, still finished second to Oakland's Tony La Russa in voting for manager of the year. There was the new front office, led by Bando, assistant vice president baseball operations Bruce Manno and player develop- ment director Fred Stanley — all in their first season in their jobs.

And of course, there were the new players.

"We tailored our ballclub to the abilities of our players," Garner said. "And everyone did a good job. We were able to communicate our ideas on playing the game a certain way. To the players' credit, they were able to adapt and went out and performed the way we wanted them to. It paid off because we had a successful season."

The Brewers know where they want to go in the future and they know who they want to build the

The 26-year-old Listach hit .290, scored 93 runs, set a club record with 54 stolen bases and was named American League rookie of the year, the first Brewers player so honored.

Another key to Milwaukee's late-season surge and another building block for the future has to be Eldred, a 6-foot-4, 25-year-old Iowan who roared through the American League the way few rookie pitchers ever have.

Eldred just missed making the big club in 1991, but in 1992, he was called up on July 15 and wasted no time proving he belonged. In one remarkable stretch from August 8 through September 29, Eldred posted 10 straight wins, tying a club record — which ironically had been set the day before by teammate Chris Bosio.

For the season, Eldred finished a glittering 11–2 with a 1.79 earned run average, a club rookie record. "He pitched the best baseball around," Garner said. "He pitched beautiful baseball."

His 1992 performance, coupled with a solid '93 season, earned Eldred a surprising milestone. He has reached 20 wins faster than any other pitcher in Major League history.

The power-hitting Vaughn finally developed into the player the Brewers had hoped he'd become. He was solid in '92 and an All-Star in 1993.

"He's finally starting to come into his own," Bando said.

Always a home run threat, Vaughn entered the 1993 season determined to hit for a higher average. "I've just tried to be more patient and wait for my pitch," said Vaughn, 28. "I guess I've matured."

club around. Among them are outfielders Greg Vaughn and Darryl Hamilton, catcher David Nilsson, infielders Pat Listach and B.J. Surhoff and pitcher Cal Eldred.

"That's the core," Bando said. "When I was in Oakland, there was a core of guys who were the key to our success and then they moved guys around them to fit the other needs."

Such a plan would seem viable in Milwaukee. Certainly the biggest surprise was shortstop Listach, who'd spent the previous four seasons in the minors and was probably planning on a fifth when he got a spring-training call to fill in for the injured Billy Spiers.

Listach had never hit higher than .272 in the minor leagues, but he flourished with the Brewers and became the consummate leadoff hitter.

"Pat had his bags packed for Denver (the Brewers' Triple A affiliate)," Garner said. "Then he went out and had a rookie of the year type season. He was a consistent solid player from Day One."

It showed as Vaughn was named the to '93 All-Star team.

Right fielder Hamilton is perhaps the player with as bright a future as any. Hamilton, 28, came up for good in 1990 and hasn't hit lower than .295 since — which is only part of a solid, all-around game that makes this guy look like an emerging star.

"Darryl is a winner," Manno said. "When you are building a winner, you look for players with good work ethics. He's a solid, everyday player. He makes good contact. He's a good outfielder. He's a good base runner. He's always prepared. That's Darryl Hamilton."

Hamilton was quietly impressive in 1992, hitting .298 with 5 homers, 62 runs batted in and 41 stolen bases, second-best on the club. And early in 1993, he set a major league record for outfielders with 541 errorless chances. He also had a streak of 235 errorless games.

"Each year I've done better, hitting for average and improving defensively," Hamilton said. "I try to improve in all aspects of my game but unfortunately, people don't look at offense and defense as going hand-in-hand. You are either considered a good defensive player or a good hitter. It felt nice to be both."

Hamilton may be the latest in a long line of Brewers who aren't particularly flashy but know how to play the game.

Of course there are others, like pitcher Jaime Navarro, who won 17 games in 1992, and catcher David Nilsson, the Australian who is still learning how good he can be.

For Bud Selig, the future is

scary and exciting at the same time. He has watched his beloved game evolve drastically over the past 25 years and, in some ways, he hasn't liked what he's seen. But baseball is still baseball to Selig and that's all that matters.

"Where would this city be without Bud?" asked longtime Brewers radio anouncer Bob Uecker.

Good question.

Actually, it would be more to the point to ask where would baseball be without Bud Selig. Through sheer perseverance, Selig and his partners were able to bring

Greg Vaughn, as his All-Star Game appearance in 1993 attests, is finally beginning to live up to his considerable potential.

(Above) Bill Wegman, after battling injuries for two seasons, finally healed up and became a quality hurler. He won 15 games with a 2.84 ERA in 1991 and came back with 13 more victories in 1992. Injuries again plagued him in 1993.

(Right) Bob Uecker, left, has been the play-by-play voice of the Brewers since 1971. His partner, Pat Hughes, has been doing Brewers broadcasts since 1984.

(Opposite) Shortstop Bill Spiers shows his athleticism is making this incredible leaping catch.

baseball back to Milwaukee. Now Selig is hoping he can keep it here.

For years, rumors have flown that Milwaukee can't sustain major league baseball any longer. The fan base isn't large enough; there are no major TV or radio dollars; there aren't enough revenue sources; the big clubs are swamping the smaller markets like Milwaukee. So on and so on.

Selig has heard it all and he can only shake his head.

"I don't know why people are pessimistic," he said. "It's like this throughout baseball, not just in Milwaukee. I'm very optimistic about the future of baseball here."

But Selig does concede one major point — the Brewers need a new stadium. And soon. Venerable County Stadium has withstood the test of time and seen its share of memories. But the old lady is showing her age.

Plans for a new facility, to be built behind the old stadium in what is now the centerfield parking lot, have been on the boards for years. The problem, though, remains who will pay for the ballpark — and how. Keys to the construction of the projected

$140 million park are the sale of stadium skyboxes and club seats, an increase in season ticket sales and more corporate sponsorships.

All aspects, say the Brewers, are critical and will eventually head toward the $105 million financing the club must arrange to build the stadium. The state of Wisconsin has approved a $35 million loan for the remainder. Brewers officials would love to see their new ball park ready for the 1996 season.

When the park (tentatively called "Brewers Stadium") is built, it will be a throwback to the golden age of baseball.

"We will have a stadium," Selig said without leaving the subject open to debate.

And who would doubt him? Everything that Selig has wanted, has needed for Milwaukee, he has somehow gotten. Will the stadium be any different? Not likely.

It sort of figures, doesn't it? This is a saga that started with Bud Selig and it's a saga that must necessarily end with him. It has been a long, storied, sometimes rocky, history for this franchise known as the Milwaukee

Outfielder Darryl Hamilton (top), short-stop Pat Listach (middle) and pitcher Cal Eldred (bottom) are three of the brightest young stars on the Brewers horizon. Hamilton may well win a batting title someday, Listach was the American League rookie of the year in 1992 and Eldred is the fastest ever to reach 20 victories. With the help of those three, and others, a World Series flag may soon be flying over a new Brewers stadium.

Brewers. It has never been easy and, with the way baseball has changed over the years, it doesn't figure to get any easier.

But the Brewers have persevered, they have ridden out the storms and they have adapted.

In his surprisingly plain office deep within County Stadium, Selig was asked one day if he had the chance to do it all again — everything — would he do it? Would the Milwaukee kid, so addicted to baseball so many years ago, still pursue the same goals that had consumed him for so many years? Would the heartaches and the disappointment and the frustration be worth it all over again?

And Selig smiled. Perhaps he was thinking about that glorious April afternoon in 1970 when, for one day, the sun never shined so brightly. Perhaps he was thinking of that October night 12 years later when his lifelong dream became a reality.

Who knows?

Maybe he was thinking about Rick Manning being booed after winning a game. Or maybe he saw Rob Deer drive that ball out of the stadium on Easter Sunday one more time. Maybe he saw the future and kids like Cal Eldred and Pat Listach and Darryl Hamilton living up to their considerable potential. Or, just maybe, he saw a World Series flag flying over his brand new stadium.

Bud Selig's smile spoke volumes. ❖

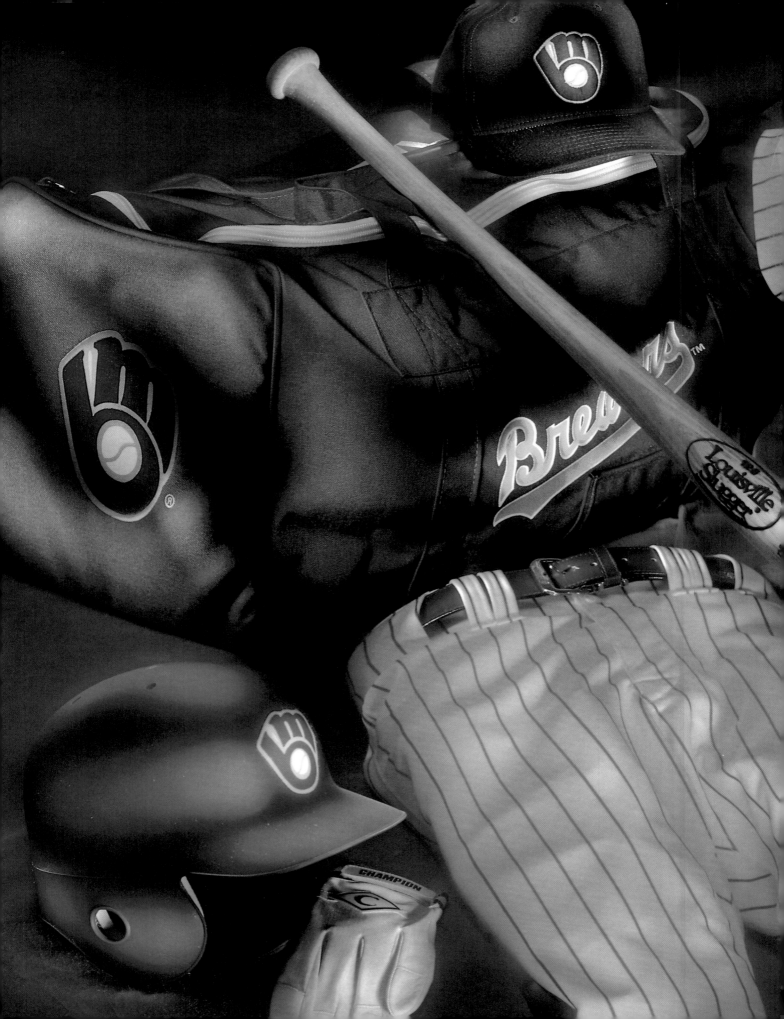

MOST VALUABLE PLAYER

1970 Tommy Harper	1982 Robin Yount
1971 Ken Sanders	1983 Cecil Cooper
1972 George Scott	1984 Jim Gantner
1973 George Scott Davey May	1985 Cecil Cooper
1974 Don Money	1986 Teddy Higuera
1975 George Scott	1987 Robin Yount
1977 Don Money	1988 Robin Yount
1978 Larry Hisle	1989 Robin Yount
1979 Sixto Lezcano	1990 Dave Parker
1980 Cecil Cooper	1991 Paul Molitor
1981 Rollie Fingers	1992 Paul Molitor

HOME RUN CHAMPION

1974 Henry Aaron	1985 Cecil Cooper
1979 Gorman Thomas	1986 Rob Deer
1980 Ben Oglivie	1987 Rob Deer
1981 Gorman Thomas	1988 Rob Deer
1982 Gorman Thomas	1989 Rob Deer
1983 Cecil Cooper	1991 Greg Vaughn
1984 Robin Yount	1992 Greg Vaughn

SEASON TEAM RECORDS — GENERAL

Category	Record	Year
Attendance, High, Home	2,397,131	1983
Attendance High, Road	2,269,077	1993
Attendance High, Total	4,284,944	1983
Doubleheaders, Best Record	6–0–4	1978
Doubleheaders, Most Wins	6	1978
Doubleheaders, Most Losses	9	1970
Doubleheaders, Worst Record	0–3–1	1990
Extra Innings, Most Wins	10	1987
Extra Innings, Most Losses	14	1982
Games Played	163	1982 1970 1969*
Games Won	95	1979 & '82
Games Lost	97	1970
Games Won, Consecutively	13	April 6–April 20, 1987 (Opening Season)
Games Won, Consecutively Two Seasons	16	1986–1987
Games Won, Consecutively, Home	10	July 8–29,1979
Games Lost Consecutively	12	May 3–May 19, 1987
Games Lost Consecutively, Home	9	July 25–August 5, 1990
Best Winning Percentage, Games Won	.590	1979
Home Record, Best	54–27 (.667)	1978
Road Record, Best	47–33 (.588)	1982
Homestand, Best	9–1 (.900)	September 18–27, 1992
Homestand, Worst	0–10 (.000) 0–8 (.000)	August 15–24, 1969* July 30–August 5, 1990
Homestand, Most Wins	11	May 12–May 28, 1981
Home Wins, Fewest	34	1971 1969*
Road Wins, Fewest	27	1970
Home Losses, Most	48	1971
Road Losses, Most	55	1970
Road Trip, Best	11–1 (.917) 6–0 (1.000)	June 4–17, 1973 April 10–15, 1987
Road Trip, Worst	0–6 (.000)	June 25–29, 1976
One Club, Most Wins vs	12	vs Toronto 1978 vs California 1971
One Club, Most Losses vs	15	vs Oakland & Baltimore 1973
One Club, Most Home Wins	9	vs Detroit 1975
One Club, Most Road Wins	6	vs Detroit 1990 vs Detroit 1982 vs Cleveland 1981 vs Minnesota 1971 vs Chicago 1970
One Run Games, Most	61	1970
One Run Games, Most Wins	33	1979
One Run Games, Most Losses	34	1971
One Run Games, Fewest Wins	12	1980
One Run Games, Fewest Losses	20	1982, 1987 & 1989
Players Used, Most	53 45	1969* 1971
Players Used, Fewest	31	1979
Righthanders, Most Wins vs	73	1979
Lefthanders, Most Wins vs	34	1982
Righthanders, Most Losses vs	77	1977
Lefthanders, Most Losses vs	36	1993, 1970 & '71 1969*
Shutouts, Both Teams, Most	36	1971
Shutouts, Most Wins	23	1971
Shutouts, Most Losses	20	1972
Shutouts, Fewest Won	2	1970
Shutouts, Fewest Losses	1	1979 & '82
Shutouts, Most vs One Team	5	vs California 1971
Shutouts, Most by Opponent	5	vs Oakland & Kansas City 1974
Non–Shutout Consecutive Games	212	Aug. 11, 1978–Sept. 29, 1979
Non–Shutout Consecutive Home Games	112	Aug. 15, 1978–April 26, 1980
Non–Shutout Consecutive Road Games	180	June 9, 1981–Sept. 11, 1983

SEASON TEAM RECORDS — BATTING

Category	Record	Year
At Bats, Most	5,733	1982
Batting Average, Highest	.280	1979
Batting Average, Lowest	.229	1971
Extra Base Hits, Most	537	1980
Grounded Into Double Plays, Most	152	1984
Grounded Into Double Plays, Fewest	98	1980
Designated Hitters,Average,Highest	.300	1991
Designated Hitters,Average, Lowest	.217	1976
Doubles, Most	298	1980
Doubles, Fewest	160	1971
Hit By Pitcher, Most	50	1989
Hit By Pitcher, Fewest	18	1982
Hits, Most	1,599	1982
Hits, Fewest	1,188	1971
Hits vs One Club, Most	192	vs Cleveland 1973
Hits vs One Club, Fewest	64	vs Kansas City 1974
Home Runs, Most	216	1982
Home Runs, Fewest	82	1992
Home Runs, Road, Most	127	1982
Home Runs, Back-to-Back	16	1982
Home Runs, Consecutive Games/15	35	June 18–July 3, 1982
Home Runs vs One Club, Most	28	vs Boston 1975 & '82
Home Runs vs One Club, Fewest	2	vs Kansas City 1974
		vs Seattle 1991
Home Runs, Grand Slams, Most	8	1980
Home Runs, Inside-the-Park, Most	3	1973 & '80
Left-On-Base, Most	1,162	1970 & '78
Left-On-Base, Fewest	1,031	1972
One-Base-Hits, Most	1,107	1991
One-Base-Hits, Fewest	901	1970
Pinch-Hits, Most	71	1970
Pinch-Hits, Fewest	4	1986
Pinch-Hit, RBI, Most	28	1970
Pinch-Hit, Home Runs, Most	6	1970
Pinch-Hit, Average, Highest	.370	1979
Pinch-Hitting Average, Lowest	.113	1985
Runs Batted In, Most	843	1982
Runs Batted In, Fewest	461	1972
Runs Scored, Most	891	1982
Runs Scored, Fewest	534	1971
Sacrifice Hits, Most	115	1970
Sacrifice Flies, Most	72	1992
Slugging Percentage, Highest	.454	1982
Slugging Percentage, Lowest	.297	1974
Stolen Bases, Most	256	1992
Stolen Bases, Caught Stealing	115	1992
Strikeouts, Most	1,040	1987
Strikeouts, Fewest	665	1983
Total Bases, Most	2,605	1982
Total Bases, Fewest	1,540	1976
Triples, Most	57	1983
Triples, Fewest	22	1972
Walks, Most	626	1969*
	598	1987
Walks, Fewest	432	1984

MOST VALUABLE PITCHER

1970 Marty Pattin	1983 Pete Ladd
1973 Jim Colborn	1985 Teddy Higuera
1974 Tom Murphy	1986 Teddy Higuera
1975 Pete Broberg	1987 Teddy Higuera
1976 Bill Travers	1988 Dan Plesac
1978 Mike Caldwell	1989 Chris Bosio
1979 Mike Caldwell	1990 Ron Robinson
1980 Moose Haas	1991 Bill Wegman
1981 Pete Vuckovich	1992 Jaime Navarro
1982 Pete Vuckovich	

ROOKIE OF THE YEAR

1971 Bill Parsons	1985 Earnest Riles
1972 Jerry Bell	1986 Dan Plesac
1973 Pedro Garcia	1987 B.J. Surhoff
1974 Robin Yount	1988 Don August
1976 Jerry Augustine	1989 Bill Spiers
1977 Moose Haas	1990 Greg Vaughn
1978 Paul Molitor	1991 Doug Henry
1983 Tom Tellmann	1992 Pat Listach
1984 Dion James	

1970

1971

1972

1973

1974

1975

1976

1977

1978

1979

1980

1981

1982

1983

1984

1985

1986

1987

1988

1989

1990

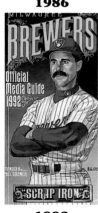

1991

1992

1993

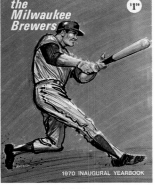

1970

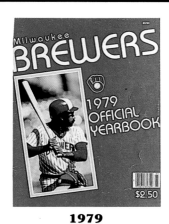

1979

1980

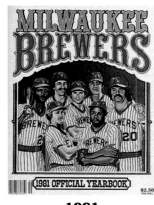

1981

1982

1983

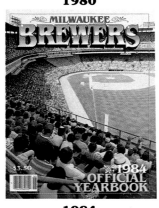

1984

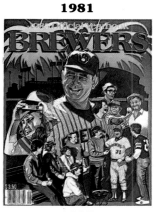

1985

1986

1987

1988

1989

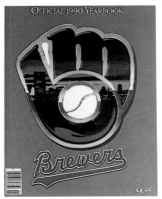

1990

1991

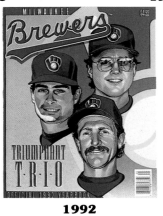

1992

211

HARVEY KUENN BATTING AWARD

1977 Cecil Cooper	1985 Paul Molitor
1978 Ben Oglivie	1986 Robin Yount
1979 Paul Molitor	1987 Paul Molitor
1980 Cecil Cooper	1988 Paul Molitor
1981 Cecil Cooper	1989 Robin Yount
1982 Robin Yount	1990 Gary Sheffield
1983 Ted Simmons	1991 Paul Molitor
1984 Robin Yount	1992 Paul Molitor

Named in the memory of Harvey Kuenn, a Milwaukee native, who coached and managed The Brewers during the 1970s and early 1980s. A lifetime .303 hitter, Kuenn led The Brewers to their first American League Pennant and to the World Series in 1982.

UNSUNG HERO AWARD

1980 Jim Gantner	1987 Dale Sveum
1981 Sal Bando	1988 Paul Mirabella
1982 Charlie Moore	1989 Chuck Crim
1984 Bill Schroeder	1990 Darryl Hamilton
1985 Frank Howard	1991 Jaime Navarro
1986 Rick Manning	1992 James Austin

SEASON TEAM RECORDS — PITCHING

Category	Record	Year
Balks, Fewest	4	1985
Balks, Most	39	1988
Complete Games, Most	62	1978
Complete Games, Fewest	13	1984
Complete Games, Consecutive	7	April 30–May 6,1979
Earned Run Average, Lowest	3.38	1971
Earned Run Average, Highest	4.62	1987
Hit Batsmen, Most	60	1993
Hit Batsmen, Fewest	19	1988
Hits, Most	1,563	1979
Hits, Fewest	1,303	1971
Home Runs, Most	175	1985
Home Runs, Fewest	99	1976
Home Runs, Home, Most	95	1969*
	81	1979
Home Runs, Home, Fewest	50	1978
One-Hit Games, Most	3	1972
Runs, Most	817	1987
Runs, Fewest	604	1992
Saves, Most	51	1988
Saves, Fewest	23	1979
Strikeouts, Most	1,039	1987
Strikeouts, Fewest	575	1980
Walks, Most	653	1969*
	624	1975
Walks, Fewest	381	1979
Wild Pitches, Most	65	1975
Wild Pitches, Fewest	29	1983
Consecutive Scoreless Innings	31	April 18–22, 1990

* Denotes records by Seattle Pilots (1969) followed by the current Milwaukee Brewers records.

SEASON TEAM RECORDS — FIELDING

Category	Record	Year
Assists, Most	1,976	1978
Assists, Fewest	1,606	1987
Chances Accepted, Most	6,434	1978
Chances Accepted, Fewest	5,923	1972
Double Plays, Most	189	1980
Double Plays, Fewest	142	1970
Errors, Most	180	1975
Errors, Fewest	89	1992
Fielding Average, Highest	.986	1992
Passed Balls	21	1969*
	20	1975
Passed Balls, Fewest	4	1978
Putouts, Most	4,402	1982
Putouts, Fewest	4,175	1972
Errorless Games, Consecutive	11	1979
Errors, Game	6	vs California 7-6-90
		vs California 7-26-78

* Denotes records by Seattle Pilots (1969) followed by the current Milwaukee Brewers records.

SEASON INDIVIDUAL RECORDS — BATTING

Category	Record	Player	Year
At Bats, Most	666	Paul Molitor	1982
Batting Average, Highest	.353	Paul Molitor	1987
Caught Stealing, Most	18	Pat Listach	1992
Doubles, Most	49	Robin Yount	1980
Extra Base Hits, Most	87	Robin Yount	1982
Games Played, Consecutively	276	Robin Yount	8-13-87/6-14-89
Games Played, Most	162	Robin Yount	1988
		Gorman Thomas	1980
Grounded Into Double Plays	26	George Scott	1975
Hit By Pitch, Most	10	Jim Gantner	1989
		Ellie Rodriguez	1973
Hits, Most	219	Cecil Cooper	1980
Hits, Players, 200 or more/Season	3	Robin Yount (210)	1982
		Cecil Cooper (205)	1982
		Paul Molitor (201)	1982
Hitting Streaks, Longest	39	Paul Molitor	1987
Hitting Streaks, Home	24	Paul Molitor	1987
Home Runs, Most	45	Gorman Thomas	1979
Home Runs, One Month, Most	12	Gorman Thomas	1979 (August)
Home Runs, Home, Most	22	Gorman Thomas	1979
Home Runs, Road, Most	26	Ben Oglivie	1980
Home Runs, Lefthanded, Most	41	Ben Oglivie	1980
Home Runs, Righthanded, Most	45	Gorman Thomas	1979
Home Runs, Grand Slams, Most	2	Rob Deer	1987
		Robin Yount	1980
		Deron Johnson	1974
		Darrell Porter	1974
		Joe Lahoud	1973
		Davey May	1973
Home Runs, Pinch-Hit, Most	2	Ken McMullen	1977
		Bobby Darwin	1975
		Bob Hansen	1974
		Andy Kosco	1971
		Max Alvis	1970
Inside-the-Park Home Runs, Most	2	Robin Yount	1979
One Base Hits, Most	157	Cecil Cooper	1980
Pinch-Hits, Most	14	Bob Hansen	1974
Runs Scored, Most	136	Paul Molitor	1982
Runs Scored, Consecutive Games	16	Paul Molitor	1987
Runs Batted In, Most	126	Cecil Cooper	1983
Runs Batted In, Lefthanded, Most	126	Cecil Cooper	1983
Runs Batted In, Righthanded, Most	123	Gorman Thomas	1979
Sacrifices, Most	19	Ron Theobald	1971
		Robin Yount	1982
Sacrifice Flies, Most	14	Dave Parker	1990
Slugging Percentage, Highest	.578	Robin Yount	1982
Stolen Bases, Most	73	Tommy Harper	1969*
	54	Pat Listach	1992
Stolen Bases, Consecutive	17	Robin Yount	8-5-88/7-19-89
Stolen Bases, Caught Stealing, Most	18	Tommy Harper	1969*
	18	Pat Listach	1993
Stolen Bases, Home Plate, Most	3	Glenn Braggs	1989
		Paul Molitor	1988
Strikeouts, Most	186	Rob Deer	1987
Total Bases, Most	367	Robin Yount	1982
Triples, Most	16	Paul Molitor	1979
Walks, Most	98	Gorman Thomas	1979

* Seattle Pilots

MICHAEL HARRISON AWARD

1976 Mike Hegan	1986 Paul Molitor
1977 Tom Ferguson	1987 Dan Plesac
1981 Willie Davis	1988 Bill Schroeder
1982 Ben Barkin	1989 Charlie O'Brien
1983 Sal Bando	1990 B.J. Surhoff
1984 Pete Vuckovich	1991 Darryl Hamilton
1985 Cecil Cooper	1992 Doug Henry

Formerly called The Good Guy Award for off-the-field contributions to the community, renamed in memory of Michael Harrison, who tragically died in an accident at County Stadium in 1992. The Award is annually presented to an individual who best exemplifies the special caring and giving personality attributed to Michael by his family and friends.

RAY SCARBOROUGH AWARD

1983 Bill Wegman	1988 Gary Sheffield
1984 Joey Meyer	1989 Chris George
1985 Billy Jo Robidoux	1990 John Byington
1986 Steve Stanicek	1991 Cal Eldred
1987 Greg Vaughn	1992 Mike Farrell

Named in memory of Ray Scarborough, former Brewers scout and assistant to the general manager, the award is given to Milwaukee's top prospect.

Brewing Some Interest

It took some time, but once The Brewers became a force in the American League, they also earned their share of national attention. Whether it was "Harvey's Wallbangers" or Robin Yount or Team Streak in 1987, The Brewers saw plenty of ink from local and national publications.

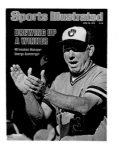

MILWAUKEE BREWERS
BASEBALL CLUB, INC.
PRESENTS

MAJOR LEAGUE BASEBALL

25¢

CHICAGO WHITE SOX
vs.
MINNESOTA TWINS

JULY 24, 1967
7:00 P.M.

1968   25¢

THE MILWAUKEE BREWERS
PRESENTS

MAJOR LEAGUE BASEBALL

FIRST WISCONSIN
CHARGE CARD

The Charge Card
for all Wisconsin's Sports

1969   25¢

THE MILWAUKEE BREWERS
PRESENTS

MILWAUKEE
BREWERS

MAJOR
LEAGUE
BASEBALL

scores
all
over the
state

FIRST WISCONSIN
CHARGE CARD

MILWAUKEE BREWERS

MILWAUKEE
BREWERS

1970
OFFICIAL SCORECARD
25¢

Today's 1971
Milwaukee
Brewers

39¢

MILWAUKEE
Brewers
1971
SCOREBOOK
35¢

...we're moving UP in 72!

The MILWAUKEE BREWERS
bring you
Major League Baseball
in WISCONSIN

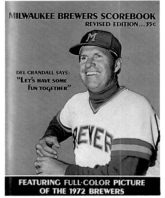

MILWAUKEE BREWERS SCOREBOOK
REVISED EDITION...35¢

DEL CRANDALL SAYS:
"LET'S HAVE SOME
FUN TOGETHER"

FEATURING FULL-COLOR PICTURE
OF THE 1972 BREWERS

LIMITED EDITION 1975 ALL-STAR SOUVENIR MAGAZINE/ MILWAUKEE $2.00

ALL-STAR GAME '75

1979 OFFICIAL PROGRAM   75¢ TAX INCL.

MILWAUKEE
BREWERS

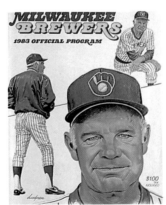

MILWAUKEE
BREWERS
1983 OFFICIAL PROGRAM

$1.00
TAX INCLUDED

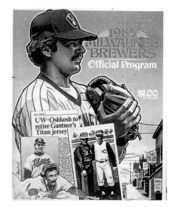

1985
MILWAUKEE
BREWERS
Official Program

$1.00

UW-Oshkosh to
retire Gantner's
Titan jersey

MILWAUKEE BREWERS
1987 Official Program
$1.25

TED
HIGUERA

MIKE
CALDWELL

THREE
OF A KIND

1988 OFFICIAL PROGRAM

Juan
Nieves

Paul
Molitor

MILWAUKEE
BREWERS

OFFICIAL 1990 PROGRAM

BREWERS

Robin Yount

MVP
Special Class

Stan Musial

Hank Greenberg

$1.50

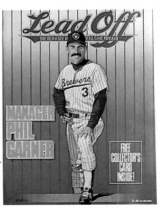

Lead Off

MANAGER
PHIL
GARNER

FREE
COLLECTOR'S
CARD
INSIDE!

BREWERS DISTINGUISHED ALUMNUS

1983	1988
Henry Aaron	Pete Vuckovich
1985	**1990**
Mike Hegan	Charlie Moore
1986	**1991**
Ken Sanders	Larry Hisle
1987	**1992**
Bill Castro	Jerry Augustine

JOHN E. FETZER AWARD

1980	1991
John E. Fetzer	Steve Palermo
1981	**1992**
Lee MacPhail	Dr. Bobby Brown

Named in memory of John E. Fetzer, former owner and chairman of the board of the Detroit Tigers for meritorious service to baseball.

ALLAN H. "BUD" SELIG PRESIDENT'S AWARD

1989	1991
Paul Molitor	Robin Yount
1990	**1992**
Rollie Fingers	Jim Gantner

Presented to an individual for meritorious service representing the Brewers on and off the field with exemplary conduct.

SEASON INDIVIDUAL RECORDS — PITCHING

Category	Record	Player	Year
Balks, Most	11	Mike Birkbeck	1988
Earned Runs, Most	127	Jaime Navarro	1993
Earned Run Average	2.37	Mike Caldwell	1978
Games, Most	83	Ken Sanders	1971
Games, Most Complete	23	Mike Caldwell	1978
Games, Most Complete, Consecutive	8	Lary Sorensen	1978
Games, Started	38	Jim Slaton	1973 & '76
Games Relieved, Most	83	Ken Sanders	1971
Games Won in Relief	14	Jim Slaton	1983
Games Won, Most	22	Mike Caldwell	1978
Games Lost, Most	20	Clyde Wright	1974
Games Won, Consecutively	10	Chris Bosio	1992
		Cal Eldred	1992
Games Lost, Consecutively	11	Chris Bosio	1988
Hit Batsmen, Most	16	Pete Broberg	1975
Hits, Most	297	Jim Colborn	1973
Home Runs, Most	35	Mike Caldwell	1983
Innings Pitched, Most	314	Jim Colborn	1973
Runs, Most	135	Jaime Navarro	1993
Saves, Consecutive Opportunities	15	Doug Henry	1991
Saves, Lefthanded Pitcher, Most	33	Dan Plesac	1989
Saves, Righthanded Pitcher, Most	31	Ken Sanders	1971
Scoreless Innings, Consecutively	32	Ted Higuera	8/26-9/11/87
Shutouts, Consecutively	3	Ted Higuera	1987
Shutouts, Most	6	Mike Caldwell	1978
Strikeouts, Lefthanded Pitcher, Most	240	Ted Higuera	1987
Strikeouts, Righthanded Pitcher, Most	180	Cal Edlred	1993
Walks, Most	106	Pete Broberg	1975
Winning Percentage	.846	Cal Eldred (11-2)	1992

*Denotes records by Seattle Pilots (1969) followed by the current Milwaukee Brewers records.

GAME TEAM RECORDS — PITCHING

Category	Record	Opponent	Date
Balks	5	at New York	4-10-88
Runs Scored	20	vs Boston	9-6-75
Runs Scored/Inning	10	vs Toronto	6-10-90
Hits	24	vs Boston	9-6-75
Hits/Innings	9	vs Seattle	7-18-91
Home Runs	6	at Detroit	9-10-86
		at Boston	5-31-80
		at Boston	5-22-77
Home Runs/Inning	4	at Detroit	9-10-86
		at Boston	5-31-86
Runs Batted In	20	vs Boston	9-6-75
Strikeouts	17	vs Toronto	6-28-87
Strikeouts, Extra Innings	17	at Chicago	5-8, 5-9-84
Walks	13	at Kansas City	6-3-79
		at New York	9-8-73
Walks, Extra Innings	18	vs Minnesota	7-19-69*

* Seattle Pilots

GAME TEAM RECORDS — BATTING

Category	Record	Opponent	Date
Runs Scored	22	at Toronto	8-28-92
Runs Scored/Inning	13	vs California	7-8-90
Hits	31	at Toronto	8-28-92
Hits/Inning	10	vs California	7-8-90
		at Boston	4-18-83
Singles	26	at Toronto	8-28-92
Doubles	9	at Seattle	9-29-92
		at Boston	4-16-90
		at Boston	10-3-87
Triples	5	at Toronto	7-30-78
Home Runs	7	at Cleveland	4-29-80
Home Runs, Inning	3	Several Times	9-12-82
Home Runs, Inning, Consecutive	3	at New York	9-12-82
		at Oakland	6-5-82
		at California	5-28-82
Total Bases	38	at Toronto	8-28-92
Runs Batted In	22	at Toronto	8-28-92
Runs Batted In/Inning	13	vs California	7-8-90
Extra Base Hits	11	at Boston	10-3-87
Left On Base	19	vs Minnesota	5-16-86
Strikeouts	17	at Texas	8-10-87
Stolen Bases	8	at Toronto	8-28-92
Walks	15	vs Seattle	7-17-91
Innings	25	at Chicago	5-8,5-9-84
Grand Slam Home Runs	2	vs Boston	4-12-80
Grand Slam Home Runs, Inning	2	vs Boston	4-12-80
Home Runs/Opener	5	vs Boston	4-10-80
Home Runs/Opener/Both Clubs	7	vs Boston	4-10-80
Runs Scored/Opener	15	at Toronto	4-9-82
Runs Scored/Opener/Opponent	12	vs California	4-7-70
Hits/Opener	16	at Toronto	4-9-82
Runs Batted In/Opener	15	at Toronto	4-9-82
Extra Base Hits/Opener	7	vs Boston	4-10-80
Total Bases/Opener	26	vs Boston	4-10-80
Winning Margin- Largest	20 (22–2)	at Toronto	8-28-92
Losing Margin- Largest	16 (19–3)	vs Oakland	5-15-85

GAME INDIVIDUAL RECORDS — PITCHING

Category	Record	Player	Opponent	Date
Balks	3	Mike Birkbeck	vs New York	4-15-88
Innings	13	Jim Colborn	at Baltimore	9-27-74
Hits	18	Bill Travers	at Cleveland	8-14-77
Runs	14	Bill Travers	at Cleveland	8-14-77
Home Runs	5	Mike Caldwell	at Boston	5-31-80
Home Runs/Inning	4	Mike Caldwell	at Boston	5-31-80
Hit Batsmen	3	Bill Wegman	vs Kansas City	4-28-92
		Pete Broberg	at Oakland	8-17-75
Strikeouts	14	Moose Haas	vs New York	4-12-78
Walks	9	Jaime Cocanower	at New York	4-13-86

ON THIS DATE

JANUARY
1978 — Brewers hire George Bamberger as field manager (Jan. 20)

1982 — Henry Aaron becomes first Brewer elected to the Hall of Fame (Jan. 13)

1991 — First BrewersFest attracts nearly 10,000 fans (Jan. 20– 21)

1992 — Rollie Fingers elected to Baseball's Hall of Fame (Jan. 7)

FEBRUARY
1986 — Explosion rocks Brewers new spring training site at Chandler (Feb. 27)

1988 — Former Manager and Coach Harvey Kuenn dies in Sun City, AZ (Feb. 28)

MARCH
1978 — Floods wash away Brewers spring training facility (March 2)

1980 — Manager George Bamberger suffers mild heart attack (March 9)

APRIL
1970 — Milwaukee awarded bankrupt Seattle Pilots (April 1)

1970 — A crowd of 37,237 welcomes baseball back to County Stadium (April 7)

1973 — A major snowstorm cancels Brewer home opener (April 10)

1974 — Robin Yount makes his major league debut (April 5)

1975 — Home Run King Hank Aaron returns to Milwaukee as a Brewer (April 11)

1978 — George Bamberger makes his managerial debut (April 7)

1980 — Sixto Lezcano hits a dramatic 9th inning game winning grand slam homer (April 10)

1987 — Juan Nieves pitches the Brewers first no-hitter (April 15)

1987 — Brewers' 9th inning rally lifts the club to its 12th straight win in a major league 13-game major league record tying start (April 19)

1990 — Brewers pitchers toss a club record third straight shutout (April 20)

1991 — Willie Randolph collects his 2,000th career hit (April 15)

1993 — Darryl Hamilton establishes an A.L. record with 541 consecutive errorless chances from the outfield (April 9)

1993 — Graeme Lloyd becomes the first Australian-born pitcher to register a major league victory (April 30)

MAY
1970 — Roberto Pena hits an inside-the-park grand slam homer (May 30)

1972 — Skip Lockwood tosses a one-hitter in Del Crandall's managerial debut (May 30)

continued next page

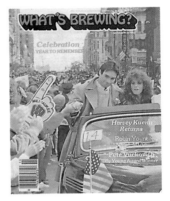

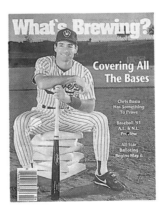

MAY cont'.

1979 — Brewers turn their last triple play (May 15)

1982 — Ted Simmons becomes first Brewer to hit a homer from both sides of the plate in a single game (May 2)

1982 — Cecil Cooper, Don Money and Gorman Thomas hit consecutive home runs in the same inning for the first time in Brewer history (May 28)

1983 — For the third time in his career Ben Oglivie hits 3 homers in a game (May 14)

1984 — Brewers and White Sox play in an American League record 25-inning marathon (May 8–9)

1991 — In what is the longest game in Brewers history at County Stadium, the club earns a 10–9 win over Chicago in 19 innings (May 1)

1991 — Paul Molitor becomes only the 4th Brewers player to hit for the cycle (May 15)

1993 — Robin Yount and George Brett become the first A.L. players with 3,000 career hits to oppose each other since 1925 (May 28)

JUNE

1973 — Brewers win their 10th straight game, a record that stood until 1987 (June 18)

1974 — Kansas City's Steve Busby tosses only no-hitter against Brewers (June 19)

1978 — Brewers win a club record 21 games for any given month (June 30)

1983 — Ted Simmons collects his 2,000th career hit (June 12)

1987 — Brewers pitching staff strikeouts out a club record 17 batters in a game (June 28)

1988 — Robin Yount becomes the third Brewer to ever hit for the cycle (June 12)

1989 — Brewers help the Toronto Blue Jays celebrate the opening of the SkyDome (June 5)

1989 — Robin Yount's club record 276 consecutive playing streak is halted (June 14)

1990 — Dave Parker collects his 2,500th career hit (June 27)

1993 — Robin Yount moves into 13th place on the All-Time Hit List (June 2)

JULY

1970 — Lew Krausse registers Brewers first shutout (July 7)

1970 — Ted Kubiak drives in a club record 7 runs in a game (July 18)

1975 — Milwaukee hosts the All-Star Game (July 15)

continued next page

GAME INDIVIDUAL RECORDS — BATTING

Category	Record	Player	Opponent	Date
At Bats	11	Cecil Cooper	at Chicago	5-8, 5-9-84
Runs Scored	4	Kevin Reimer	vs Oakland #2	8-24-93
		Paul Molitor (7)	at Oakland	6-16-92
		B.J. Surhoff (2)	at Toronto	8-28-92
		Dante Bichette	at Boston	6-28-92
		Kevin Seitzer	at Toronto	8-28-92
		Robin Yount (2)	at Chicago	6-12-88
		Juan Castillo	at Seattle	5-1-87
		Ted Simmons (2)	vs California	7-22-85
		Jim Gantner	at Minnesota	7-27-83
		Charlie Moore	at Toronto	4-9-82
		Larry Hisle (3)	at Cleveland	4-29-80
		Cecil Cooper	vs Baltimore	4-14-79
		Sixto Lezcano	at Kansas City	7-13-78
		Russ Snyder	at Chicago	4-12-70
Hits	6	Kevin Reimer	vs Oakland #2	8-24-93
		John Briggs	at Cleveland	8-4-73
Doubles	3	B.J. Surhoff	vs New York	9-15-93
		Pat Listach	at Toronto	8-6-93
		Robin Yount (4)	at Seattle	9-29-92
		Dave Parker	at Boston	4-16-90
		Paul Molitor (2)	at Seattle	9-8-89
		Greg Brock	at Boston	10-3-87
		Don Money	at Chicago	5-15-82
		Gorman Thomas (2)	at Toronto #2	7-13-80
		Sixto Lezcano	vs New York	7-28-79
		Kurt Bevacqua	at Oakland	6-2-75
Triples	2	Tom Brunansky	vs Cleveland	5-15-93
		Paul Molitor (2)	at Minnesota	8-1-92
		Franklin Stubbs	at Kansas City	7-23-91
		Robin Yount	vs New York	7-28-86
		Randy Ready	at Kansas City	9-7-85
		Rick Manning (2)	at Cleveland	5-30-86
		Ted Simmons	at Minnesota	5-26-84
		Ted Savage	vs Oakland	9-15-70
Home Runs	3	Dale Sveum	vs California	7-17-87
		Ben Oglivie (3)	vs Boston	5-14-83
		Paul Molitor	at Kansas City	5-12-82
		Cecil Cooper	vs New York	7-27-79
Home Runs, Left & Righthanded	1	Dale Sveum	at Chicago	6-12-88
		Dale Sveum	vs California	7-17-87
		Ted Simmons	at Minnesota	5-2-82
Total Bases	13	Paul Molitor	at Kansas City	5-12-82
Runs Batted In	7	Ted Kubiak	at Boston	7-18-70
Sacrifice Hits	3	Bobby Coluccio	vs New York	5-3-75
Strikeouts	5	Joey Meyer	at California	9-20-88
		Jeffrey Leonard	vs Cleveland	8-24-88
		Rob Deer	at Chicago#1	8-8-87
Strikeouts, Extra Innings	5	Gorman Thomas	vs Cleveland	7-13-79
Walks	4	Greg Vaughn (2)	vs New York	9-15-93
		Kevin Seitzer	vs Oakland	8-25-93
		Paul Molitor	vs Chicago	5-1-91
		Rob Deer	vs Cleveland	4-16-89
		Danny Walton	at Kansas City	5-22-70
Stolen Bases	4	John Jaha	at Baltimore	9-11-92
		Tommy Harper	at Chicago	6-18-69

continued next page

GAME INDIVIDUAL RECORDS — BATTING CONT'.

Category	Record	Player	Opponent	Date
Stolen Bases, Inning	3	Paul Molitor	vs Oakland	7-26-87
Hitting for the Cycle	1	Paul Molitor	at Minnesota	5-15-91
		Robin Yount	at Chicago	6-12-88
		Charlie Moore	at California	10-1-80
		Mike Hegan	at Detroit	9-3-76
Inside the Park, Home Run	1	Robin Yount	at Kansas City (6)	5-3-90
		Mike Felder	vs Baltimore	9-26-89
		Ben Oglivie	at Oakland	9-26-80
		Jim Gantner	at Seattle	9-13-80
		John Briggs	vs Boston #2	6-19-73
		Davey May	at Minnesota	6-11-73
		Roberto Pena	vs Detroit	5-30-70
Inside the Park, Grand Slam	1	Ben Oglivie	at Oakland	9-26-80
		Roberto Pena	vs Detroit	5-30-70

BREWERS YEAR-BY-YEAR

AMERICAN LEAGUE WEST

Year	Manager	Record	Pct.	GB/A	Pos.	Attend.
1970	Dave Bristol	65–97	.401	-33	4T	933,690
1971	Dave Bristol	69–92	.429	-32	6	731,531

AMERICAN LEAGUE EAST

Year	Manager	Record	Pct.	GB/A	Pos.	Attend.
1972	Dave Bristol	65–91	.417	-21	6	600,440
1973	Del Crandall	74-88	.457	-23	5	1,092,158
1974	Del Crandall	76–86	.460	-15	5	955,741
1975	Del Crandall	68–94	.420	-28	5	1,213,357
1976	Alex Grammas	66–95	.410	-32	6	1,012,164
1977	Alex Grammas	67–95	.414	-33	6	1,114,938
1978	George Bamberger	93–69	.574	-6	3	1,601,406
1979	George Bamberger	95–66	.590	-8	2	1,918,343
1980#	George Bamberger	86–76	.531	-17	3	1,857,408
1981*	Buck Rodgers	62–47	.560	+1	1	878,432
1982+	Buck Rodgers–Harvey Kuenn	95–67	.586	+1	1	1,978,896
1983	Harvey Kuenn	87–75	.537	-11	5	2,397,131
1984	Rene Lachermann	67–94	.416	-36.5	7	1,608,509
1985	George Bamberger	71–90	.441	-28	6	1,360,265
1986%	George Bamberger– Tom Trebelhorn	77–84	.451	-18	6	1,265,041
1987	Tom Trebelhorn	91–71	.562	-7	3	1,909,244
1988	Tom Trebelhorn	87–75	.537	-2	3T	1,923,238
1989	Tom Trebelhorn	81–81	.500	-8	4	1,970,735
1990	Tom Trebelhorn	74–88	.457	-14	6	1,752,900
1991	Tom Trebelhorn	83–79	.513	-8	4	1,478,814
1992	Phil Garner	92–70	.568	-4	2	1,857,314
1993	Phil Garner	69–93	.426	-26	7	1,688,080

Buck Rodgers, Acting Manager (39–31/.557)

* Shortened Seasom (First Half: 31–25; Second Half: 31–22)

+ Harvey Kuenn, Interim Manager (72–43/.626)

% Tom Trebelhorn, replaces George Bamberger, September 26 (6–3/.667)

ON THIS DATE CONT'.

JULY

1976 — Henry Aaron hits his 755th and last home run (July 20)

1982 — Milwaukee hits its 35th homer in 15 game span, setting a record (July 3)

1983 — Brewers post their best ever homestand, winning 10 of 12 games (July 24)

1987 — Paul Molitor sets a club record by stealing 3 bases in one inning (July 26)

1988 — Dan Plesac earns his 9th straight save in as many opportunities (July 19)

1989 — Robin Yount hits his 200th career home run (July 31)

1990 — The Brewers rally from a 7–0 deficit to score a 20–7 victory. Milwaukee scores a club record 13 runs in the 5th inning when 18 batters go to the plate. (July 8)

1991 — Paul Molitor collects his 2,000th career hit (July 30)

1992 — Paul Molitor's single to center-field at Kansas City in Game One of a doubleheader makes Milwaukee's trio of Molitor–Robin Yount–Jim Gantner baseball's all-time hitting teammates. (July 5)

AUGUST

1971 — Skip Lockwood is the last Brewer pitcher to hit a homer in a game (Aug. 11)

1973 — Johnny Briggs collects a Brewer record 6 hits in a game (Aug. 4)

1979 — Gorman Thomas set a club record with 12 homers in a month (Aug. 29)

1981 — Following a 56-day strike baseball resumes play with rescheduled All-Star Game (Aug. 10)

1982 — After splitting a doubleheader with Cleveland, the Brewers move into first place in the A.L. East for good (Aug. 1)

1982 — Milwaukee acquires Don Sutton from Houston (Aug. 31)

1987 — Paul Molitor extends his hitting streak to a club record 39 straight games (Aug. 25)

1991 — Tom Trebelhorn becomes first Brewers manager to get 400 career wins (Aug. 30)

1992 — By stealing 8 bases in a game, Brewers set a new club record (Aug. 5)

1992 — Brewers set an American League record with 31 hits in a game (Aug. 28)

1992 — Milwaukee establishes a new club standard with 22 runs against Toronto (Aug. 28)

SEPTEMBER

1970 — Tommy Harper joins elite 30–30 club after hitting his 30th homer to go along with 38 stolen bases (Sept. 22)

continued next page

SEPTEMBER cont'.

1973 — Jim Colborn becomes the Brewers first 20-game winner (Sept. 1)

1974 — Jim Colborn pitches a club record 13 innings in a game (Sept. 27)

1976 — Mike Hegan is the first Brewer to hit for the cycle (Sept. 3)

1978 — Mike Caldwell sets a club record with his 22nd victory of the year (Sept. 30)

1979 — Brewers win the club record 95th game (Sept. 29)

1983 — Brewers establish an all-time Milwaukee sports attendance record with 2.4 million fans (Sept. 29)

1986 — Teddy Higuera is the last Brewer pitcher to win 20 games in a season (Sept. 25)

1986 — Tom Trebelhorn becomes Brewer manager (Sept. 26)

1989 — Dan Plesac sets a club record with his 33rd save of the year (Sept. 30)

1992 — Robin Yount becomes only the 17th player in major league history to collect 3,000 hits (Sept. 9)

1992 — Chris Bosio becomes the first Brewers pitcher to win 10 straight decisions (Sept. 24)

1992 — Cal Eldred equals the club record by winning his 10th straight decision (Sept. 29)

1992 — Milwaukee posts its finest record for the month, going 20–7, as it challenges Toronto for the American League East pennant. (Sept. 30)

OCTOBER

1972 — Brewers acquire Don Money in a multi-player trade with Philadelphia (Oct. 31)

1976 — Hank Aaron singles in his last major league at bat (Oct. 3)

1980 — Charlie Moore hits for the cycle (Oct. 1)

1981 — Brewers qualify for post-season action (Oct. 2)

1982 — Brewers win A.L. East pennant in season finale at Baltimore (Oct. 3)

1982 — Cecil Cooper's 2-run single in the 7th inning lifts the Brewers to a come from behind victory over California capturing A.L. crown (Oct. 10)

1982 — Milwaukee loses World Series to St. Louis (Oct. 17)

1991 — Sal Bando becomes Brewers senior vice president—Baseball Operations (Oct. 8)

1991 — Phil Garner is named the Brewers new manager (Oct. 30)

1992 — Brewers finish the season with their 4th best record ever (92–70) good for 2nd place in the American League East (Oct. 4)

continued next page

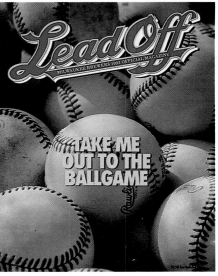

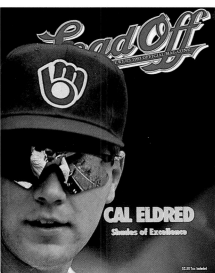

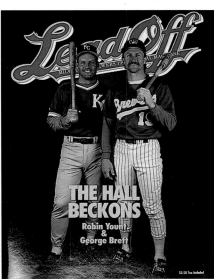

NOVEMBER

1976 — Milwaukee signs free-agent Sal Bando (Nov. 17)

1977 — Brewers hire Harry Dalton as executive vice president-general manager (Nov. 20)

1977 — Milwaukee selects new logo in statewide contest (Nov. 28)

1978 — George Bamberger earns "A.L. Manager of the Year" honors (Nov. 7)

1981 — Rollie Fingers is voted "A.L. Cy Young Award" winner (Nov. 3)

1981 — Rollie Fingers earns "A.L. Most Valuable Player" award (Nov. 24)

1982 — Pete Vuckovich recognized as the "A.L. Cy Young Award" winner (Nov. 3)

1982 — Robin Yount named "A.L. Most Valuable Player" (Nov. 10)

1989 — Robin Yount becomes only the 3rd player ever to earn MVP honors at 2 positions (Nov. 20)

1992 — Pat Listach earns the "American League Rookie of the Year Award" (Nov. 4)

1992 — Brewers lose pitchers Darren Holmes and Jeff Tabaka and infielder Jim Tatum in the National League expansion draft. (Nov. 17)

DECEMBER

1976 — Brewers complete a trade with Boston for Cecil Cooper (Dec. 6)

1977 — Milwaukee swings a deal with Detroit for Ben Oglivie (Dec. 9)

1980 — In a multi-player trade, Brewers land Ted Simmons, Pete Vuckovich and Rollie Fingers from St. Louis (Dec. 10)

1989 — Brewers sign free-agent Dave Parker (Dec. 3)

1990 — Brewers sign free-agent Franklin Stubbs (Dec. 5)

1992 — Long time Brewers fan favorite Paul Molitor, signs as free agent with Toronto (Dec. 7)

COACHES

Cal Ermer	1970–1971	First Base
Roy McMillan	1970–1972	Third Base
Jackie Moore	1970–1972	Bullpen
Wes Stock	1970–1972	Pitching
Harvey Kuenn	1972–1982*	Batting
Joe Nossek	1973–1975	Third Base
Bob Shaw	1973	Pitching
Jim Walton	1973–1975	First Base
Al Widmar	1974	Pitching
Ken McBride	1975	Pitching
Hal Smith	1976–1977	Bullpen
Jimmy Bragen	1976–1977	Third Base
Cal McLish	1976–1982	Pitching
Frank Howard	1977–1980; 1985	First Base, Batting
Buck Rodgers	1978–1980*	Third Base
Larry Haney	1978–1991	Bullpen, Pitching
Ron Hansen	1981–1983	First Base
Harry Warner	1981–1982	Third Base
Pat Dobson	1982–1984	Pitching
Dave Garcia	1983–1984	Third Base
Tom Trebelhorn	1984; 1986*	First Base, Third Base
Tony Muser	1985–1989	Third Base, Batting
Andy Etchebarren	1985–1991	First Base, Bench
Herm Starrette	1985–1986	Pitching
Dave Hilton	1987–1988	First Base
Chuck Hartenstein	1987–1989	Pitching
Duffy Dyer	1989–Present	Third Base
Don Baylor	1990–1991	Batting
Ray Burris	1990–1991	Bullpen
Fred Stanley	1991	Infield
Bill Castro	1992–Present	Bullpen
Mike Easler	1992	Batting
Tim Foli	1992–Present	First Base, Infield
Don Rowe	1992–Present	Pitching
Gene Clines	1993–Present	Batting

* Became Brewers Manager

BOARD OF DIRECTORS

Edmund B. Fitzgerald
Ralph Evinrude
Charles A. Krause
Bernard S. Kubale
Allan H. "Bud" Selig
Everett G. Smith
Roswell N. Stearns
Carlton P. Wilson

CLUB OFFICERS

Sal Bando
Jim Baumer
Robert C. Cannon
John Cordova
Richard W. Cutler
Harry Dalton
Jeff Eisenberg
Tom Ferguson
Al Goldis
Dick Hackett
Bill Haig
Dick Hoffmann
Frank Lane
Gabe Paul, Jr.
Laurel Prieb
Bob Schoenbachler
Allan H. "Bud" Selig
Wendy Selig-Prieb
Carlton P. Wilson
Jim Wilson

GENERAL MANAGERS

Marvin Milkes	1970
Frank Lane	1971–72
Jim Wilson	1973–74
Jim Baumer	1975–77
Harry Dalton	1978–91
Sal Bando	1992–Present

BREWERS MANAGERS

Dave Bristol
1970–1972

Del Crandall
1972–1975

Alex Grammas
1976–1977

George Bamberger
1978–80, 1985–86

Bob "Buck" Rodgers
1980–1982

Harvey Kuenn
1982–1983

Rene Lachemann
1984

Tom Trebelhorn
1986–1991

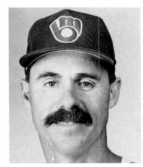
Phil Garner
1992–Present

MANAGERS CAREER RECORDS

Rank		W	L	Pct.
1	Harvey Kuenn	159	118	.574
2	Bob "Buck" Rodgers	101	78	.564
3	George Bamberger	377	351	.518
4	Tom Trebelhorn	422	397	.515
5	Phil Garner	161	163	.497
6	Del Crandall	273	339	.446
7	Rene Lachemann	67	94	.416
8	Alex Grammas	133	190	.412
9	Dave Bristol	144	209	.408

BREWERS RADIO BROADCASTERS

Merle Harmon	1970–1979
Tom Collins	1970–1972
Eddie Doucette	1970
Bob Uecker	1972–Present
Lorn Brown	1980–1981
Dwayne Mosley	1982–1983
Pat Hughes	1984–Present

BREWERS TELEVISION ANNOUNCERS

Dan O'Neill	1970
Merle Harmon	1970–72, 1976–79
Tom Collins	1970–74
Jim Irwin	1971, 1975
Bob Uecker	1972, 1976–80
Johnny Logan	1973
Eddie Doucette	1973–74
Gary Bender	1975
Ray Scott	1976–77
Mike Hegan	1978–80, 1982–88
Lorn Brown	1980
Steve Shannon	1981–86
Kent Derdivanis	1981
Jim Paschke	1987–91
Pete Vuckovich	1989–91
Rory Markas	1992–Present
Del Crandall	1992–Present

BREWERS PLAYER ROSTER BY NUMBER

0

Franklin Stubbs

00

Jeffrey Leonard

1

Ted Kubiak
Bernie Smith
Jose Cardenal
Dick Schofield
Tim Johnson*
Tim Nordbrook
Ernest Riles
Gary Sheffield*
Alex Diaz*

2

Ted Savage
Bob Heise
Bob Sheldon
Lenn Sakata*
Ed Romero*
Randy Ready
Edgar Diaz
William Suero
Jose Valentin*

3

Bernie Smith*
John Felske*
Joe Lahoud
Deron Johnson
Gorman Thomas*
Ed Kirkpatrick
Billy Jo Robidoux*
Juan Castillo*
Dante Bichette*

4

Tim Johnson*
Mike Hegan*
Paul Molitor

5

Phil Roof
George Scott
Jamie Quirk*
Tony Muser
Ned Yost
Doug Loman
B.J. Surhoff

6

Mike Hershberger
Carl Taylor
Ellie Rodriguez
Mike Hegan*
Sal Bando
Bill Spiers*
Andy Allanson

7

Russ Synder
Frank Tepedino
Ron Clark
Syd O'Brien
Don Money
Paul Householder

8

Mike Hegan*
Rob Ellis
Jack Heidemann
Jim Wynn
Andy Etchebarren
Ray Fosse*
John Poff
Bob Skube*
Rob Picciolo
Jim Sundberg
Dante Bichette*
Dickie Thon

9

Rich Rollins
Tito Francona
Gary Sutherland
Billy Conigliaro
Pedro Garcia
Tim Johnson*
Larry Hisle
Jim Adduci*
Greg Brock
Bill Spiers*

10

Max Alvis
Andy Kosco
Tommie Reynolds
Art Kusnyer
Bob McClure
Juan Nieves*
Gus Polidor*

11

John Kennedy
Davey May
Kurt Bevacqua
Jim Rosario
Sixto Lezcano*
Steve Brye
Jeff Yurak
Vic Harris*
Ed Romero*
Charlie O'Brien*
Rick Cerone
Mike Young*
LaVel Freeman
Greg Vaughn*
Gary Sheffield*
Dave Nilsson*

12

Danny Walton
Johnny Briggs
Bernie Carbo
Bobby Darwin
Larry Haney
Scott Fletcher

13

Steve Barber
Ray Fosse*
Roy Howell
Billy Jo Robidoux*
Dave Nilsson*
Bill Doran

14

John Felske*
Ollie Brown
Felipe Alou
Bob Hansen*
Jim Wolhford
Dion James
Jim Adduci*
Jim Paciorek
Gus Polidor*
Rick Dempsey

15

Jerry McNertney
Darrell Porter
Cecil Cooper

16

Gus Gil
Ron Theobald
Ken Barry
Sixto Lezcano*
Marshall Edwards
Juan Castillo*
Mike Felder
Kevin Brown*
Pat Listach

17

Pete Koegel
Steve Bowling
Paul Ratliff
Joe Azcue
Bobby Mitchell
Bob Hansen*
Ken McMullen
Jim Gantner

18

Tom Hausman
Barry Cort
Bob Galasso*
Danny Darwin
Darryl Hamilton*
Jim Olander
Alex Diaz*
Tom Brunansky

19

Bob Burda
Rick Auerbach
Robin Yount

20

Wayne Comer
Ken Sanders
Lafayette Currence
Gorman Thomas*
Don Sutton*
Rick Waits*
Ray Burris*
Juan Nieves*
Willie Randolph
Kevin Seitzer

21

Tommy Harper
Curt Motton
Jack Lind
John Vukovich
Lenn Sakata*
Bob Sheldon
Buck Martinez
Don Sutton*
Bill Schroeder
Dennis Powell
Jerry Reuss
Jeff Kaiser
Cal Eldred

22

Fred Stanley
Tom Matchick
Bernie Smith*
Brock Davis
Charlie Moore
Steve Stanicek
Charlie O'Brien*
George Canale*
Candy Maldonado
Tom Lampkin

23

Ray Peters
Carlos Velazquez
Eduardo Rodriguez
Reggie Cleveland*
Ted Simmons
Joey Meyer
Greg Vaughn*

24

Lew Krausse*
Ken Brett
Ben Oglivie
Darryl Hamilton*

25

John Gelnar
Bob Reynolds
Frank Linzy
Bill Travers
Reggie Cleveland*
Bobby Clark
Mark Clear
Dave Engle
Ricky Bones

26

Bobby Coluccio
Bill Sharp
Dick Davis
Kevin Bass
Bob Skube*
Andy Beene
Willie Lozado
Brian Giles
Glenn Braggs
Tim McIntosh
Juan Bell

27

Bob Locker
Roger Miller
Chris Short
Andy Replogle
Thad Bosley
Pete Ladd
Jim Adduci*
Paul Mirabella
Neal Heaton
Joe Kmak

28

Sandy Valdespino
Roberto Pena
Wilbur Howard
Von Joshua
Jamie Easterly
Rick Manning
Jeff Peterek
Odell Jones
Tom Filer*
Franklin Stubbs*
Doug Henry

29

Larry Bearnarth
Jim Lonborg
Ed Sprague
Gary Beare*
Lance Rautzhan
Mark Brouhard
Chris Bosio
Kevin Reimer

BREWERS PLAYER ROSTER BY NUMBER

30	35	40	44	49
Lew Krausse*	John Morris	Floyd Wicker	Hank Allen	George Lauzerique
Moose Haas	Earl Stephenson	Jerry Bell	Gorman Thomas*	Floyd Weaver
Steve Kiefer	Dick Selma	Pete Broberg	Henry Aaron[2]	Dick Ellsworth
Terry Francona	Bill Castro	Sam Hinds	(Retired)	Ray Newman
Bob Sebra	Randy Lerch	Willie Mueller*		Pat Osburn
Kevin Brown*	Doug Jones	Dave LaPoint		Fred Holdsworth
Willie Randolph*	Narciso Elvira	John Flinn	**45**	Frank DiPino
Bruce Ruffin		Bob Gibson		Fred Martinez
Matt Mieske	**36**	Mike Birkbeck*	Dave Baldwin*	Tom Candiotti
		Darren Holmes	Larry Anderson*	Teddy Higuera
31	Steve Hovley	Mike Ignasiak*	Rich Folkers	
	Archie Reynolds		Bob Galasso*	**50**
Tommy Harper*	Al Downing	**41**	Dan Boitano*	
Jim Gantner*	Mark Bomback		Buster Keaton	Gary Timberlake
Gary Beare*	Rick Waits*	Jim Slaton	Rob Deer	Pete Vuckovich
Donnie Moore	Carlos Ponce	Jack Lazorko	Edwin Nunez*	Matt Maysey
Alex Madrid	Brad Komminsk	Mike Birkbeck*		
Jaime Navarro	Ray Krawczyk	Ray Searage	**46**	**51**
	Tony Fossas	Mark Knudson		
32	Mike Capel	Edwin Nunez*	Dave Baldwin*	Brad Lesley
	Mike Fetters		Ken Reynolds	Jim Tatum
Gene Brabender		**42**	Jerry Augustine	Josias Manzanillo
Bill Voss	**37**		Bill Wegman	
Chuck Crim		Skip Lockwood		**52**
John Jaha	Jim Kern	Tom Murphy	**47**	
	Dan Plesac	Willie Mueller*		Bill Parsons
33	Graeme Lloyd	Jaime Cocanower*	Bob Humphreys	Carlos Maldonado*
		Tom Tellmann	Ed Farmer	Mike Boddicker
Marty Pattin	**38**	Dave Huppert	Dwight Bernard	
Mike Ferraro		James Austin	Jaime Cocanower*	**53**
Bob Gardner	Bob Meyer		Bill Krueger	
Tom Bianco	Marcelino Lopez	**43**	Jesse Orosco	Michael Ignasiak*
Doc Medich	Bill Champion*			
Jamie Nelson	Clyde Wright	John O'Donoghue	**48**	**54**
Jay Aldrich*	John Henry Johnson*	Gary Ryerson		
George Canale*	Don August	Larry Anderson*	Wayne Twitchell	Jose Valentin*
Ron Robinson	Angel Miranda	Rick Austin	Jim Colborn	
Troy O'Leary		Randy Stein	Mike Caldwell	**59**
	39	Paul Mitchell	Tim Leary*	
34		Chuck Porter	Brian Clutterbuck	Chris George
	Bob Bolin	Dave Stapleton	Ray Burris*	
Greg Goossen	John Felske*	Mike Young*	Tom Edens	
Jim Hannan	Bill Champion*	Randy Veres	Julio Machado	
Chuck Taylor	Danny Thomas	Jim Hunter	Carlos Maldonado*	
Al Yates	Danny Frisella	Mark Kiefer		
Kevin Kobel	Lary Sorensen			
Ray Sadecki	Dan Boitano*			
Ed Romero*	Paul Hartzell			
Rollie Fingers[1]	Len Barker			
Mark Ciardi	Tim Leary*			
Billy Bates	Tom Filer*			
John Henry Johnson*	Dave Parker			
Mark Lee	Matias Carrillo			
(Retired)	Rafael Novoa			

Wore More Than One Number

[1] *Retired Uniform Number — Rollie Fingers*
[2] *Retired Uniform Number — Henry Aaron*

BREWERS OFF-THE-FIELD DIRECTORY 1970–1994

A

Warren Abramson, Administration
Jan Ackerman, Broadcast Operations
John Adam, Trainer
Rod Adel, Groundskeeper
Keith Askenaski, Public Relations

B

Marlene Babinec, Public Relations
George Bamberger, Baseball Operations
Sal Bando, Vice President, Baseball
  Operations
Paul Baniel, Accounting
Jimmy Bank, Traveling Secretary
John Barnes, Ticketing
Robbin Barnes, Community Relations
Jim Bathey, Ticketing
Jim Baumer, Vice President, Baseball
  Operations
Don Baylor, Baseball Operations
Sharon Berner, Executive Secretary
Marilyn Betthauser, Accounting
Bob Betts, Public Address Announcer
Betsy Billerbeck, Public Relations
Mary Bliss, Public Relations
Alice Boettcher, Ticketing
Ron Borchardt, Stadium Operations
Ted Borkowski, Stadium Operations
Irene Bolton, Executive Secretary
Jeri Brenneis, Ticketing
Karen Brooks, Marketing
Lisa Brzeski, Executive Secretary
Liz Burke, Public Relations
Mary Burns, Legal
Ray Burris, Baseball Operations

C

Ken Califano, Baseball Operations
Geoff Campion, Ticketing
Marion Chandler, Baseball Operations
Frank Charles, Organist
Len Ciborosky, Broadcast Operations
Viola Coleman, Personnel
Dick Collenberg, Hospitality
Steve Comte, Ticketing
John Cordova, Vice President, Marketing
Cheryl Corso, Accounting
John Counsell, Community Relations
Gary Crites, Employee Assistance
John Crowe, Trainer
Hiram Cuevas, Baseball Operations
Bill Curley, Public Relations

D

Kathy Dailey, Broadcast Operations
Harry Dalton, Vice President, Baseball
  Operations
Linda Daute, Stadium Operations
Doug Decauter, Baseball Operations
Diane DeNomie, Executive Secretary
Mike Downs, Community Relations
Nancy Dressel, Ticketing
Emerson Dugar, Ticketing
Dan Duquette, Baseball Operations

E

Jeff Eisenberg, Vice President, Ticketing
Steve Ethier, Traveling Secretary

F

Criag Fahey, Baseball Operations
Kathy Feilen, Stadium Operations
Tom Ferguson, Vice President,
  Administration
Dee Fondy, Baseball Operations
Dick Foster, Baseball Operations
Jane Fox, Community Relations
Freddie Frederico, Trainer
Jake Frego, Marketing
Andy Friedrich, Broadcast Operations
Rich Fromstein, Ticketing

G

Arnold Garrett, Maintenance
Tom Gausden, Baseball Operations
-eleni- Gerasopoulos, Public Relations
Harry Gill, Groundskeeper
Jeff Gittins, Ticketing
Tad Gittins, Ticketing
Shirley Glitz, Baseball Operations
Al Goldis, Baseball Operations
Sean Grabowski, Public Address
  Announcer
Betty Grant, Receptionist
John Grant, Stadium Operations
David Green, Ticketing
Jon Greenberg, Public Relations
Matt Groniger, Ticketing
Mykky Gustin, Ticketing
Dr. Gary N. Guten, Team Physician

H

Betsy Hackett, Ticketing
Dick Hackett, Vice President, Ticketing
Bill Haig, Vice President, Broadcast
  Operations
Mike Hamacher, Ticketing
Larry Haney, Baseball Operations
Ross Harmsen, Ticketing
Christ Harrison, Administration
Debbie Harvey, Stadium Operations
Wendy Heiser, Stadium Operations
Dick Hoffmann, Vice President, Finance
Jack Hutchinson, Stadium Operations
Bob Humphreys, Baseball Operations

J

Danny Jackson, Maintenance
Dr. Paul Jacobs, Team Physician
Sandra Jaje, Ticketing
Mike Jakubowski, Stadium Operations
Bridgette Johnson, Personnel
Kim Johnson, Ticketing

K

Lori Keck, Executive Secretary
Art Keefe, Public Relations
Carol Keller, Stadium Operations
Chuck Klein, Stadium Operations
Donna Koepke, Personnel
Cheryl Konkel, Baseball Operations
Carla Koplin, Baseball Operations
Dan Krautkramer, Information Services
Brian Krueger, Accounting
Jim Ksicinski, Administration
Harvey Kuenn, Baseball Operations

L

Karen Leaders, Receptionist
Charlotte Leque, Accounting

M

Pat Mack, Stadium Operations
Christal Mahnke, Receptionist
Bruce Manno, Asst. Vice President,
    Baseball Operations
Claudia Manno, Public Relations
Scott Martens, Baseball Operations
Lew Matlin, Baseball Operations
Cindy Matlock, Executive Secretary
Bob Mattick, Baseball Operations
Crystal McCollum, Personnel
Carol McInnis, Stadium Operations
Dave Mellor, Groundskeeper
Aleta Mercer, Broadcast Operations
Val Meyer, Photographer
Joe Migliaccio, Administration
Tony Migliaccio, Equipment Manager
Beverly Mirek, Stadium Operations
Ron Modra, Photographer
Kathy Moeschberger, Accounting
Liz Morgan, Public Relations

N

Mary Jo Nennig, Broadcast Operations
Brenda North, Stadium Operations

O

Toby Oldham, Baseball Operations
Cheryl Oren, Marketing
Mike Osenga, Public Relations
Linda Osgaard, Stadium Operations
Tom Osowski, Ticketing

P

Mark Paget, Ticketing
J.D. Patton, Baseball Operations
Gabe Paul, Jr., Vice President, Stadium
    Operations
Andy Perry, Administration
Terry Ann Peterson, Stadium Operations
Tom Pilak, Stadium Operations
Ray Poitevint, Baseball Operations
Syl Polk, Stadium Operations
Tonya Powell, Ticketing
Roxanne Prah, Ticketing
Donna Presser, Ticketing
Al Price, Trainer
Laurel Prieb, Vice President,
    Communications

Q

Bob Quinn, Baseball Operations

R

Pepi Randolph, Legal
Curt Rayer, Trainer
Lynn Renelt, Accounting
Dean Rennicke, Gold Club
Gail Rex, Accounting
Dan Richlen, Marketing
Cindy Robers, Stadium Operations
Pat Rogo, Maintenance
Sandra Ronback, Executive Secretary
Linda Rosiak, Stadium Operations
Bernie Rupp, Maintenance
Steve Rymkus, Ticketing

S

Dan Sandler, Administration
Sue Sawall, Stadium Operations
Ray Scarborough, Baseball Operations
John Schaller, Public Address Announcer
Judd Schemmel, Baseball Operations
Karen Schlenvogt, Accounting
Stephaine Schmidt, Broadcast Operations
Michelle Schneider, Accounting
Bob Schoenbachler, Accounting
Diane Schoenfeld, Ticketing
Sandy Schubert, Stadium Operations
Cathy Schwab, Accounting
Bill Sears, Public Relations
Wes Seidel, Accounting
Allan H. "Bud" Selig, President, Chief
    Executive Officer
Wendy Selig-Prieb, Vice President, Legal
Walter Shannon, Baseball Operations
Tony Siegle, Baseball Operations
Gail Simon, Administration
Tom Skibosh, Public Relations
Matt Slater, Baseball Operations
Brian Small, Baseball Operations
Troy Smith, Groundskeeper
Kent Sommerfeld, Broadcast Operations
Denny Sommers, Baseball Operations
George Spelius, Baseball Operations
Fred Stanley, Baseball Operations
Barb Stark, Baseball Operations
Donna Stark, Public Relations
Kay Stark, Receptionist
Herman Starrette, Baseball Operations
Tiffany Stone, Marketing
Larry Stoudt, Photographer
Joyce Stube, Baseball Operations
Eddie Stumpf, Consultant
Bob Sullivan, Equipment Manager
Dr. Dennis Sullivan, Team Physician

T

Chuck Tanner, Baseball Operations
Jerry Topczewski, Ticketing
Tim Trovato, Ticketing
Gerry Tucker, Accounting
Maimi Tucker, Administration
Jack Turan, Groundskeeper

V

Gary Vanden Berg, Groundskeeper
Tim Van Wagoner, Marketing

W

Chuck Ward, Stadium Operations
Ed Wellskopf, Hospitality
Marty Wellskopf, Hospitality
Vern Wendland, Stadium Operations
Al Widmar, Baseball Operations
Barb Wilfert, Personnel
Bridgette Wynn, Ticketing

Z

Linda Zech, Stadium Operations
Paul Zellner, Maintenance
Mario Ziino, Public Relations
Fran Zugel, Maintenance

MILWAUKEE BREWERS FIRSTS

GENERAL FIRSTS

Game	April 7, 1970	vs California Angels	at County Stadium
Road Game	April 10, 1970	at Chicago White Sox	Comiskey Park
Night Game	April 13, 1970	at Oakland A's	Oakland-Alameda County Coliseum
Sunday Game	April 12, 1970	at Chicago White Sox	Comiskey Park
Home Attendance	April 7, 1970	vs California Angels	at County Stadium, 37,237
Road Attendance	April 10, 1970	at Chicago White Sox	Comiskey Park, 1,036
Victory	April 11, 1970	at Chicago White Sox	Comiskey Park, 8-4
Home Victory	May 6, 1970	vs Boston Red Sox	at County Stadium, 4-3
Extra Inning Game	April 18, 1970	at California Angels	Anaheim Stadium, 5-4 Loss/10 Innings
Extra Inning Game At Home	May 9, 1970	vs Washington Senator	at County Stadium, 3-2 Win /10 Innings
Shutout - Loss	April 7, 1970	vs California Angels	at County Stadium, 12-0
Shutout - Win	July 7, 1970	vs Chicago White Sox	at County Stadium, 1-0
1-0 Game - Win	July 7, 1970	vs Chicago White Sox	at County Stadium
1-0 Game - Loss	August 23, 1970	at Detroit Tigers	Tiger Stadium
Doubleheader	April 12, 1970	at Chicago White Sox (Sweep: Victory/ 5-2 and 16-2)	Comiskey Park
Manager	Dave Bristol		
Youngest Player	Robin Yount	18 Years,7 Months,11 Days (First Game: April 5, 1974)	
Oldest Player	Henry Aaron	42 Years, 7 Months, 29 Days (Last Game: October 4, 1976)	
Trade	April 4, 1970	Acquired Max Alvis and Russ Snyder from Cleveland Indians for Roy Foster and Frank Coggins	

INDIVIDUALS — BATTING

Batter	April 7, 1970	Tommy Harper vs California Angels (Opposing Pitcher: Andy Messersmith) at County Stadium (First Inning)
Hit	April 7, 1970	Steve Hovley vs California Angels (Andy Messersmith) at County Stadium (2nd Inning)
Double	April 8, 1970	Tommy Harper vs California Angels (Tom Murphy) at County Stadium
Triple	May 8, 1970	Russ Snyder at New York Yankees (Dave Burbach) Yankee Stadium
Home Run	April 11, 1970	Danny Walton at Chicago White Sox (Billy Wynne) Comiskey Park (6th Inning)
Grand Slam Home Run	May 30, 1970	Roberto Pena vs Detroit Tigers (Les Cain) at County Stadium
Run Scored	April 8, 1970	Tommy Harper vs California Angels at County Stadium (7th Inning)
Runs Batted In	April 8, 1970	Russ Snyder vs California Angels at County Stadium (7th Inning)
Stolen Base	April 8, 1970	Tommy Harper vs California Angels at County Stadium
Fielding Error	April 7, 1970	Russ Snyder vs California Angels at County Stadium

MILWAUKEE BREWERS FIRSTS

INDIVIDUALS — PITCHING

Pitcher	April 7, 1970	Lew Krausse vs California Angels at County Stadium (3 IP, 3 H, 4 R, 4 ER, 1 BB, 1 K)
Decision	April 7, 1970	Lew Krausse vs California Angels at County Stadium (3 IP, 3 H, 4 R, 4 ER, 1 BB, 1 K), 12–0 Loss
Victory	April 11, 1970	John O'Donoghue at Chicago White Sox, Comiskey Park (2 IP, 0 H, 0 R, 0 ER, 0 BB, 3 K), 8–4, In Relief
Victory By A Starter	April 12, 1970	Lew Krausse at Chicago White Sox, Comiskey Park (5.1 IP, 4 H, 2 R, 2 ER, 4 BB, 1 K), 5–2 First Game/Doubleheader
Complete Game	April 12, 1970	George Lauzerique at Chicago White Sox, Comiskey Park (9 IP, 9 H, 2 R, 2 ER, 1 BB, 7 K), 16–2 Win Second Game/Doubleheader
Save	April 11, 1970	Bob Locker at Chicago White Sox, Comiskey Park (1 IP, 0 H, 0 R, 0 ER, 0 BB, 0 K), 8–4 Win
Home Run Allowed	April 10, 1970	Gene Brabender at Chicago White Sox (Bobby Knoop) Comiskey Park (4.1 IP, 7 H, 5 R, 3 ER, 1 BB, 3 K), 5–4 Loss
Shutout	July 7, 1970	Lew Krausse vs Chicago White Sox at County Stadium (9 IP, 4 H, 0 R, 0 ER, 1 BB, 6 K), 1–0 Win
No-Hitter	April 15, 1987	Juan Nieves at Baltimore Orioles, Memorial Stadium (9 IP, 0 H, 0 R, 0 ER, 5 BB, 7 K), 7–0 Win
One Hitter	May 30, 1972	Skip Lockwood vs New York Yankees at County Stadium (9 IP, 1 H, 1 R, 1 ER, 6 BB, 4 K), 3–1 Win
Two-Hitter	July 28, 1970	Al Downing vs Washington Senators at County Stadium (9 IP, 2 H, 1 R, 1 ER, 6 BB, 6 K), 5–1 Win

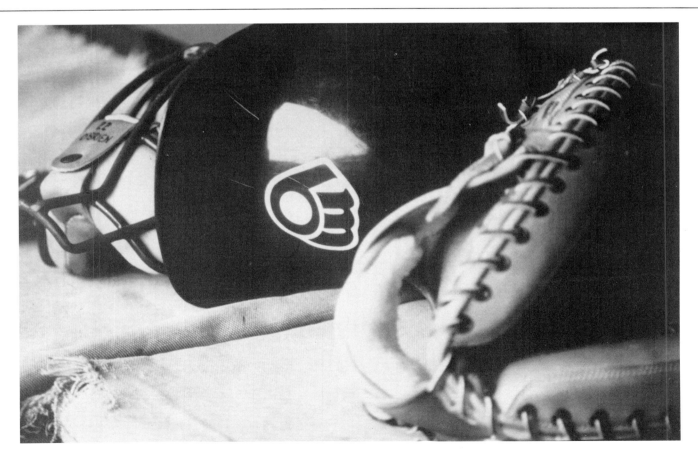

BREWERS ALL-TIME TOP TEN

SINGLE SEASON & CAREER
1970–93

GAMES

	Season				Career	
1.	Yount	162	1988	1.	Yount	2858
2.	Thomas	162	1982	2.	Molitor	1856
3.	Gantner	161	1983	3.	Gantner	1801
4.	Yount	161	1976	4.	Cooper	1490
5.	Yount	160	1989	5.	Moore	1283
6.	Yount	160	1984	6.	Money	1196
7.	Cooper	160	1983	7.	Oglivie	1149
8.	Molitor	160	1982	8.	Thomas	1102
9.	Cooper	160	1977	9.	Surhoff	945
10.	Garcia	160	1973	10.	Lezcano	785

AT BATS

	Season				Career	
1.	Molitor	666	1982	1.	Yount	11008
2.	Molitor	665	1991	2.	Molitor	7520
3.	Cooper	661	1983	3.	Gantner	6189
4.	Cooper	654	1982	4.	Cooper	6019
5.	Cooper	643	1977	5.	Money	4330
6.	Yount	638	1976	6.	Oglivie	4136
7.	Yount	635	1987	7.	Moore	3926
8.	Yount	635	1982	8.	Thomas	3544
9.	Cooper	631	1985	9.	Surhoff	3335
10.	Money	629	1974	10.	Scott	3009

RUNS

	Season				Career	
1.	Molitor	136	1982	1.	Yount	1632
2.	Molitor	133	1991	2.	Molitor	1275
3.	Yount	129	1982	3.	Cooper	821
4.	Yount	121	1980	4.	Gantner	726
5.	Molitor	115	1988	5.	Money	596
6.	Molitor	114	1987	6.	Oglivie	567
7.	Cooper	106	1983	7.	Thomas	524
8.	Yount	105	1984	8.	Moore	441
9.	Cooper	104	1982	9.	Scott	402
10.	Harper	104	1970	10.	Surhoff	380

HITS

	Season				Career	
1.	Cooper	219	1980	1.	Yount	3142
2.	Molitor	216	1991	2.	Molitor	2281
3.	Yount	210	1982	3.	Cooper	1815
4.	Cooper	205	1982	4.	Gantner	1696
5.	Cooper	203	1983	5.	Money	1168
6.	Molitor	201	1982	6.	Oglivie	1144
7.	Yount	198	1987	7.	Moore	1029
8.	Molitor	195	1992	8.	Surhoff	896
9.	Yount	195	1989	9.	Scott	851
10.	Molitor	194	1989	10.	Thomas	815

DOUBLES

	Season				Career	
1.	Yount	49	1980	1.	Yount	613
2.	Yount	46	1982	2.	Molitor	405
3.	Cooper	44	1979	3.	Cooper	345
4.	Yount	42	1983	4.	Gantner	262
5.	Molitor	41	1991	5.	Money	215
6.	Molitor	41	1987	6.	Oglivie	194
7.	Yount	40	1992	7.	Moore	177
8.	Cooper	39	1986	8.	Thomas	172
9.	Simmons	39	1983	9.	Surhoff	157
10.	Yount	38	1989	10.	Scott	137
11.	Surhoff	38	1993			

TRIPLES

	Season				Career	
1.	Molitor	16	1979	1.	Yount	126
2.	Molitor	13	1991	2.	Molitor	86
3.	Yount	12	1982	3.	Moore	42
4.	Yount	11	1988	4.	Gantner	38
5.	Yount	10	1983	5.	Cooper	33
6.	Yount	10	1980	6.	Lezcano	22
7.	Yount	9	1989	7.	Oglivie	21
8.	Yount	9	1987	8.	Money	20
9.	Yount	9	1979	9.	Surhoff	19
10.	Cooper	8	1986	10.	Scott	19

HOME RUNS

	Season				Career	
1.	Thomas	45	1979	1.	Yount	251
2.	Oglivie	41	1980	2.	Thomas	208
3.	Thomas	39	1982	3.	Cooper	201
4.	Thomas	38	1980	4.	Oglivie	176
5.	Scott	36	1975	5.	Molitor	160
6.	Oglivie	34	1982	6.	Deer	137
7.	Hisle	34	1978	7.	Money	134
8.	Deer	33	1986	8.	Scott	115
9.	Cooper	32	1982	9.	Vaughn	102
10.	Thomas	32	1978	10.	Lezcano	102

RBI

	Season				Career	
1.	Cooper	126	1983	1.	Yount	1406
2.	Thomas	123	1979	2.	Cooper	944
3.	Cooper	122	1980	3.	Molitor	790
4.	Cooper	121	1982	4.	Oglivie	685
5.	Oglivie	118	1980	5.	Thomas	605
6.	Hisle	117	1978	6.	Gantner	568
7.	Yount	114	1982	7.	Money	529
8.	Thomas	112	1982	8.	Scott	463
9.	Scott	109	1975	9.	Surhoff	429
10.	Simmons	108	1983	10.	Moore	401

AVERAGE

	Season				Career	
1.	Molitor	.353	1987	1.	Molitor	.303
2.	Cooper	.352	1980	2.	Cooper	.302
3.	Yount	.331	1982	3.	Hamilton	.297
4.	Randolph	.327	1991	4.	Yount	.285
5.	Molitor	.325	1991	5.	Scott	.283
6.	Molitor	.322	1979	6.	Oglivie	.277
7.	Lezcano	.321	1979	7.	Hisle	.276
8.	Molitor	.320	1992	8.	Lezcano	.275
9.	Yount	.318	1989	9.	Gantner	.274
10.	Molitor	.315	1989	10.	Sheffield	.271

STOLEN BASES

	Season				Career	
1.	Listach	54	1991	1.	Molitor	412
2.	Molitor	45	1987	2.	Yount	271
3.	Hamilton	41	1992	3.	Gantner	137
4.	Molitor	41	1988	4.	Harper	136
5.	Molitor	41	1983	5.	Felder	108
6.	Molitor	41	1982	6.	Hamilton	95
7.	Harper	38	1970	7.	Surhoff	95
8.	Felder	34	1987	8.	Cooper	77
9.	Molitor	34	1980	9.	Listach	72
10.	Molitor	33	1979	10.	Money	66

PITCHING
1970–93

APPEARANCES

	Season					Career	
1.	Sanders	83	1971		1.	Plesac	365
2.	Crim	76	1989		2.	Slaton	364
3.	Crim	70	1988		3.	McClure	352
4.	Murphy	70	1974		4.	Crim	332
5.	Henry	68	1992		5.	Augustine	279
6.	McClure	68	1977		6.	Castro	253
7.	Crim	67	1990		7.	Haas	245
8.	Crim	66	1991		8.	Caldwell	239
9.	Lee	62	1991		9.	Rodriguez	235
10.	Sanders	62	1972		10.	Bosio	212

GAMES STARTED

	Season					Career	
1.	Slaton	38	1973		1.	Slaton	268
2.	Eldred	36	1993		2.	Haas	231
3.	Sorensen	36	1978		3.	Caldwell	217
4.	Colborn	36	1973		4.	Higuera	193
5.	Pattin	36	1971		5.	Wegman	193
6.	Higuera	35	1987		6.	Bosio	163
7.	Slaton	35	1974		7.	Travers	157
8.	Parsons	35	1971		8.	Navarro	141
9.	Krausse	35	1971		9.	Colborn	140
10.	Navarro	34	1992		10.	Sorensen	119
11.	Navarro	34	1991				
12.	Navarro	34	1993				

VICTORIES

	Season					Career	
1.	Caldwell	22	1978		1.	Slaton	117
2.	Higuera	20	1986		2.	Caldwell	102
3.	Colborn	20	1973		3.	Higuera	93
4.	Higuera	18	1987		4.	Haas	91
5.	Vuckovich	18	1982		5.	Wegman	68
6.	Sorensen	18	1978		6.	Bosio	67
7.	Navarro	17	1992		7.	Travers	65
8.	Caldwell	17	1982		8.	Navarro	58
9.	Eldred	16	1993		9.	Colborn	57
10.	Bosio	16	1992		10.	Augustine	55
11.	Higuera	16	1988				

E.R.A.

	Season*					Career	
1.	Eldred	1.79	1992		1.	Sanders	2.22
2.	Caldwell	2.37	1978		2.	Fingers	2.54
3.	Higuera	2.45	1988		3.	Tellmann	2.68
4.	Higuera	2.79	1985		4.	Castro	2.96
5.	Travers	2.81	1976		5.	Plesac	3.21
6.	Lonborg	2.83	1972		6.	Linzy	3.27
7.	Wegman	2.84	1991		7.	Murphy	3.29
8.	Robinson	2.91	1990		8.	Higuera	3.46
9.	Bosio	2.95	1989		9.	Crim	3.47
10.	Krausse	2.95	1971		10.	Colborn	3.65

COMPLETE GAMES

	Season					Career	
1.	Caldwell	23	1978		1.	Caldwell	85
2.	Colborn	22	1973		2.	Slaton	69
3.	Sorensen	17	1978		3.	Haas	55
4.	Caldwell	16	1979		4.	Colborn	51
5.	Sorensen	16	1979		5.	Higuera	50
6.	Higuera	15	1986		6.	Sorensen	50
7.	Travers	15	1976		7.	Travers	44
8.	Wright	15	1974		8.	Wegman	38
9.	Higuera	14	1987		9.	Bosio	32
10.	Haas	14	1980		10.	Augustine	27

SHUTOUTS

	Season					Career	
1.	Caldwell	6	1978		1.	Slaton	19
2.	Pattin	5	1971		2.	Caldwell	18
3.	Caldwell	4	1979		3.	Higuera	12
4.	Colborn	4	1973		4.	Travers	10
5.	Slaton	4	1971		5.	Haas	8
6.	Parsons	4	1971		6.	Bosio	8
7.	Navarro	3	1992		7.	Colborn	7
8.	Higuera	3	1987		8.	Sorensen	7
9.	Haas	3	1983		9.	Navarro	6
10.	Caldwell	3	1982		10.	Augustine	6

INNINGS

	Season					Career	
1.	Colborn	314.0	1973		1.	Slaton	2025.0
2.	Caldwell	293.1	1978		2.	Caldwell	1603.0
3.	Slaton	293.0	1976		3.	Haas	1542.0
4.	Sorensen	280.2	1978		4.	Higuera	1321.1
5.	Slaton	276.1	1973		5.	Wegman	1295.2
6.	Pattin	264.2	1971		6.	Bosio	1190.0
7.	Wegman	261.2	1992		7.	Colborn	1118.0
8.	Higuera	261.2	1987		8.	Travers	1068.0
9.	Caldwell	258.0	1982		9.	Navarro	953.1
10.	Eldred	258.0	1993		10.	Augustine	944.0

STRIKEOUTS

	Season					Career	
1.	Higuera	240	1987		1.	Higuera	1046
2.	Higuera	207	1986		2.	Slaton	929
3.	Higuera	192	1988		3.	Haas	800
4.	Eldred	180	1993		4.	Bosio	749
5.	Bosio	173	1989		5.	Wegman	587
6.	Pattin	169	1971		6.	Caldwell	540
7.	Nieves	163	1987		7.	Colborn	497
8.	Pattin	161	1972		8.	McClure	495
9.	Bosio	150	1987		9.	Navarro	459
10.	Haas	146	1980		10.	Travers	459

SAVES

	Season					Career	
1.	Plesac	33	1989		1.	Plesac	133
2.	Sanders	31	1971		2.	Fingers	97
3.	Plesac	30	1988		3.	Henry	61
4.	Henry	29	1992		4.	Sanders	61
5.	Fingers	29	1982		5.	Castro	44
6.	Fingers	28	1981		6.	Crim	42
7.	Ladd	25	1983		7.	Murphy	41
8.	Plesac	24	1990		8.	McClure	34
9.	Plesac	23	1987		9.	Ladd	33
10.	Fingers	23	1984		10.	Rodriguez	30

WINNING PCT.

	Season					Career	
1.	Eldred	.846(11-2)	1992		1.	Eldred	.617(29-18)
2.	Haas	.813(13-3)	1983		2.	Higuera	.612(93-59)
3.	Vuckovich	.778(14-4)	1988		3.	Vuckovich	.606(40-26)
4.	Vuckovich	.750(18-6)	1982		4.	Nieves	.561(32-23)
5.	Bosio	.727(16-6)	1992		5.	Caldwell	.560(102-80)
6.	Caldwell	.727(16-6)	1979		6.	Navarro	.537(58-50)
7.	Caldwell	.710(22-9)	1978		7.	Champion	.537(22-19)
8.	Robinson	.706(12-5)	1990		8.	Haas	.535(91-79)
9.	Slaton	.700(14-6)	1983		9.	August	.531(34-30)
10.	Wegman	.682(15-7)	1991		10.	Sorensen	.531(52-46)

Earned Run Average (Season) reflects only starting pitchers.

April 6, 1993
BREWERS vs ANGELS
Anaheim Stadium

16	Pat Listach	SS
24	Darryl Hamilton	RF
19	Robin Yount	CF
23	Greg Vaughn	LF
18	Tom Brunansky	DH
5	B.J. Surhoff	3B
32	John Jaha	1B
8	Dickie Thon	2B
27	Joe Kmak	C
46	Bill Wegman	RHP

April 6, 1992
TWINS vs BREWERS
County Stadium

4	Paul Molitor	DH
24	Darryl Hamilton	RF
5	B.J. Surhoff	C
23	Greg Vaughn	LF
19	Robin Yount	CF
0	Franklin Stubbs	1B
20	Kevin Seitzer	3B
17	Jim Gantner	2B
12	Scott Fletcher	SS
46	Bill Wegman	RHP

April 5, 1983
BREWERS vs ANGELS
Anaheim Stadium

4	Paul Molitor	3B
19	Robin Yount	SS
15	Cecil Cooper	1B
23	Ted Simmons	C
24	Ben Oglivie	LF
20	Gorman Thomas	CF
13	Roy Howell	DH
22	Charlie Moore	RF
17	Jim Gantner	2B
20	Don Sutton	RHP

April 9, 1982
BREWERS vs BLUE JAYS
Exhibition Stadium

4	Paul Molitor	3B
22	Charlie Moore	C
15	Cecil Cooper	1B
24	Ben Oglivie	LF
20	Gorman Thomas	CF
9	Larry Hisle	DH
19	Robin Yount	SS
29	Mark Brouhard	RF
17	Jim Gantner	2B
50	Pete Vuckovich	RHP

April 8, 1991
BREWERS vs RANGERS
Arlington Stadium

4	Paul Molitor	DH
19	Robin Yount	CF
11	Gary Sheffield	3B
28	Franklin Stubbs	1B
22	Candy Maldonado	LF
3	Dante Bichette	RF
5	B.J. Surhoff	C
17	Jim Gantner	2B
6	Bill Spiers	SS
41	Mark Knudson	RHP

April 9, 1990
WHITE SOX vs BREWERS
County Stadium

11	Gary Sheffield	3B
5	B.J. Surhoff	C
19	Robin Yount	CF
39	Dave Parker	DH
45	Rob Deer	RF
9	Greg Brock	1B
26	Glenn Braggs	LF
2	Kiki Diaz	SS
34	Billy Bates	2B
29	Chris Bosio	RHP

April 11, 1981
BREWERS vs INDIANS
Cleveland Stadium

4	Paul Molitor	CF
19	Robin Yount	SS
15	Cecil Cooper	1B
24	Ben Oglivie	LF
23	Ted Simmons	C
9	Larry Hisle	DH
20	Gorman Thomas	RF
7	Don Money	3B
17	Jim Gantner	2B
48	Mike Caldwell	LHP

April 10, 1980
RED SOX vs BREWERS
County Stadium

4	Paul Molitor	2B
15	Cecil Cooper	1B
26	Dick Davis	DH
24	Ben Oglivie	LF
20	Gorman Thomas	CF
16	Sixto Lezcano	RF
7	Don Money	3B
19	Robin Yount	SS
22	Charlie Moore	C
41	Jim Slaton	RHP

April 3, 1989
BREWERS vs INDIANS
Cleveland Stadium

14	Gus Polidor	3B
1	Gary Sheffield	SS
19	Robin Yount	CF
45	Rob Deer	RF
26	Glenn Braggs	LF
30	Terry Francona	1B
23	Joey Meyer	DH
5	B.J. Surhoff	C
17	Jim Gantner	2B
38	Don August	RHP

April 4, 1988
BREWERS VS ORIOLES
Memorial Stadium

4	Paul Molitor	DH
19	Robin Yount	CF
5	B.J. Surhoff	C
9	Greg Brock	1B
45	Rob Deer	LF
26	Glenn Braggs	RF
1	Ernest Riles	3B
17	Jim Gantner	2B
7	Dale Sveum	SS
49	Teddy Higuera	LHP

April 5, 1979
BREWERS vs YANKEES
Yankee Stadium

4	Paul Molitor	DH
7	Don Money	2B
15	Cecil Cooper	1B
9	Larry Hisle	LF
16	Sixto Lezcano	RF
6	Sal Bando	3B
19	Robin Yount	SS
20	Gorman Thomas	CF
22	Charlie Moore	C
25	Bill Travers	RHP

April 7, 1978
ORIOLES vs BREWERS
County Stadium

4	Paul Molitor	SS
7	Don Money	3B
6	Sal Bando	DH
9	Larry Hisle	LF
16	Sixto Lezcano	RF
15	Cecil Cooper	1B
20	Gorman Thomas	CF
21	Lenn Sakata	2B
8	Andy Etchebarren	C
46	Jerry Augustine	LHP

April 7, 1987
RED SOX vs BREWERS
County Stadium

4	Paul Molitor	3B
19	Robin Yount	CF
26	Glenn Braggs	RF
9	Greg Brock	1B
13	Billy Jo Robidoux	DH
45	Rob Deer	LF
21	Bill Schroeder	C
17	Jim Gantner	2B
7	Dale Sveum	SS
49	Teddy Higuera	LHP

April 6, 1986
BREWERS VS WHITE SOX
Comiskey Park

16	Mike Felder	LF
19	Robin Yount	CF
4	Paul Molitor	3B
13	Billy Jo Robidoux	1B
1	Ernest Riles	SS
45	Rob Deer	RF
7	Paul Householder	DH
17	Jim Gantner	2B
11	Rick Cerone	C
49	Teddy Higuera	LHP

April 7, 1977
BREWERS vs YANKEES
Yankee Stadium

28	Von Joshua	CF
19	Robin Yount	SS
15	Cecil Cooper	1B
6	Sal Bando	3B
16	Sixto Lezcano	RF
7	Don Money	2B
5	Jamie Quirk	DH
14	Jamie Wohlford	LF
22	Charlie Moore	C
25	Bill Travers	RHP

April 10, 1976
YANKEES vs BREWERS
County Stadium

22	Charlie Moore	LF
7	Don Money	3B
5	George Scott	1B
15	Darrell Porter	C
44	Henry Aaron	DH
16	Sixto Lezcano	CF
26	Bill Sharp	RF
19	Robin Yount	SS
9	Pedro Garcia	2B
41	Jim Slaton	LHP

April 9, 1985
WHITE SOX vs BREWERS
County Stadium

4	Paul Molitor	3B
19	Robin Yount	LF
15	Cecil Cooper	1B
24	Ben Oglivie	RF
23	Ted Simmons	DH
5	Doug Loman	CF
21	Bill Schroeder	C
17	Jim Gantner	2B
26	Brian Giles	SS
30	Moose Haas	RHP

April 3, 1984
BREWERS vs ATHLETICS
Alameda County Stadium

2	Randy Ready	3B
17	Jim Gantner	2B
19	Robin Yount	SS
15	Cecil Cooper	1B
23	Ted Simmons	DH
24	Ben Oglivie	LF
8	Jim Sundberg	C
22	Charlie Moore	RF
28	Rick Manning	CF
20	Don Sutton	RHP

April 8, 1975
BREWERS vs RED SOX
Fenway Park

26	Bobby Coluccio	CF
12	Johnny Briggs	LF
44	Henry Aaron	DH
5	George Scott	1B
7	Don Money	3B
15	Darrell Porter	C
16	Sixto Lezcano	RF
9	Pedro Garcia	2B
19	Robin Yount	SS
41	Jim Slaton	RHP

April 5, 1974
RED SOX vs BREWERS
County Stadium

7	Don Money	3B
16	Ken Berry	DH
11	Davey May	CF
5	George Scott	1B
12	Johnny Briggs	LF
15	Darrell Porter	C
26	Bobby Coluccio	RF
9	Pedro Garcia	2B
19	Robin Yount	SS
48	Jim Colborn	RHP

STARTING LINEUPS CONT'.

April 6, 1973
BREWERS vs RED SOX
Fenway Park

11	Davey May	CF
19	Rick Auerbach	SS
12	Johnny Briggs	LF
5	George Scott	1B
7	Don Money	3B
14	Ollie Brown	DH
3	Gorman Thomas	RF
6	Ellie Rodriguez	C
9	Pedro Garcia	2B
48	Jim Colborn	RHP

April 15, 1972
BREWERS vs INDIANS
Cleveland Stadium

19	Rick Auerbach	SS
11	Davey May	CF
12	Johnny Briggs	1B
5	George Scott	3B
3	Joe Lahoud	LF
32	Bill Voss	RF
17	Paul Ratliff	C
16	Ron Theobald	2B
52	Bill Parsons	RHP

April 7, 1971
BREWERS vs TWINS
Metropolitan Stadium

31	Tommy Harper	3B
8	Mike Hegan	1B
11	Davey May	CF
10	Andy Kosco	LF
3	Bernie Smith	RF
28	Roberto Pena	SS
5	Phil Roof	C
1	Ted Kubiak	2B
33	Marty Pattin	RHP

April 7, 1970
ANGELS vs BREWERS
County Stadium

21	Tommy Harper	2B
7	Russ Snyder	CF
8	Mike Hegan	1B
12	Danny Walton	LF
15	Jerry McNertney	C
36	Steve Hovley	RF
10	Max Alvis	3B
1	Ted Kubiak	SS
24	Lew Krausse	RHP

BREWERS ALL-STARS 1970–1993

POSITION PLAYERS

Year	Name/Position	AB	R	H	RBI	Highlights
1993	Greg Vaughn, OF	1	1	1	0	1Bs & scores in the 7th
1992	Paul Molitor, 1B	2	0	1	0	PH 1B in 6th/ SO in 8th
1991	Paul Molitor, 3B	0	0	0	0	1st to reach on C Inf.
1990	Dave Parker, DH			– DNP –		1st Brewers DH in ASG
1988	PAUL MOLITOR, 2B	3	0	0	0	Last Brewers starter
1985	Cecil Cooper, 1B	0	0	0	0	PH BB in 5th
	Paul Molitor, 3B	1	0	0	0	SO in 7th/Moves to CF in 9th
1984	Jim Sundberg, C	1	0	0	0	FO in 7th
1983	Cecil Cooper, 1B	1	1	1	0	PH 1B & scores in 8th
	Ben Oglivie, OF	1	0	0	0	SO in 7th
	TED SIMMONS, C	2	0	0	0	GO in 1st/FO in 3rd
	*ROBIN YOUNT, SS	2	1	0	1	SF in 2nd/BB & scores on Fred Lynn grand slam HR in 3rd
1982	@CECIL COOPER, 1B	2	0	1	0	IF 1B in 1st/SO in 4th
	Ben Olgivie, OF	1	0	0	0	FO in 9th
	ROBIN YOUNT, SS	3	0	0	0	SO in 1st/BB in 4th/ FC in 6th/FC in 8th
1981	Ted Simmons, C	1	0	1	1	PH run scoring 1B in 6th
	Gorman Thomas, OF	1	0	0	0	PH FO in 4th
1980	Cecil Cooper, 1B	1	0	0	0	GDP in 7th
	PAUL MOLITOR, 2B			– DNP –		Injury
	+BEN OGLIVIE, OF	2	0	0	0	BB in 2nd/SO in 3rd/GO in 5th
	Robin Yount, SS	2	0	0	0	GO in 5th/FO in 7th
1979	Cecil Cooper, 1B	0	0	0	0	PH BB in 2nd
1978	Larry Hisle, OF	1	0	1	0	1st Brewers hit: PH 1B in 7th
	DON MONEY, 2B	2	0	0	0	1st Brewers starter
1977	Don Money, 2B			– DNP –		Injury
1976	Don Money, 2B	1	0	0	0	FO in 9th
1975	Henry Aaron, OF	1	0	0	0	PH FO in 2nd
	George Scott, 1B	2	0	0	0	SO in 6th/SO in 9th
1974	Don Money, 3B			– DNP –		
	Darrell Porter, C			– DNP –		
1973	Davey May, OF	2	0	0	0	FO's in 5th & 8th
1972	Ellie Rodriguez, C			– DNP –		
1970	Tommy Harper, 3B	0	0	0	0	PR in 5th

TOTALS: 33 Position Players 36 3 6 2 .167 Batting Average

PITCHERS

Year	Name	IP	H	R	ER	BB	SO	Highlights
1989	Dan Plesac	0.0	1	0	0	0	0	Von Hayes 1B in 8th
1988	Dan Plesac	0.1	0	0	0	0	1	SO Darryl Strawberry
1987	Dan Plesac	1.0	0	0	0	0	1	Pitches the 8th
1986	Teddy Higuera	3.0	1	0	0	1	2	Follows Roger Clemens
1982	Rollie Fingers	1.0	2	0	0	0	0	Pitches the 8th
1981	Rollie Fingers	1.0	2	2	2	2	0	Takes the loss
1978	Lary Sorensen	3.0	1	0	0	0	0	1st Brewers Pitcher APP
1977	#Jim Slaton			– DNP –				
1976	Bill Travers			– DNP –				
1973	Jim Colborn			– DNP –				
1971	Marty Pattin			– DNP –				

TOTALS: 11 Pitchers 9.1 7 2 2 3 4 1.92 Earned Run Average

KEY

CAPS: Starter   * Top Vote-getter   + Replaced Jim Rice in 1980
Replaced Don Money   @ Replaced Rod Carew

APP: Apperance   **BB:** Base on Balls   **CF:** Center Field
DH: Designated Hitter   **DNP:** Did Not Play   **FC:** Fielders Choice
FO: Fly Out   **GDP:** Grounded Double Play   **GO:** Ground Out
HR: Home Run   **IF:** Infield   **PH:** Pinch Hit
PR: Pinch Run   **SF:** Sacrifice Fly   **SO:** Strike Out
1B: Single   **2B:** Double   **3B:** Triple

1981
AMERICAN LEAGUE
EASTERN DIVISION SERIES

MILWAUKEE BREWERS
vs
NEW YORK YANKEES

For the first time in major league history, a divisional playoff series was established because of the split season. In the American League East, New York, winners of the first half title took on Milwaukee, the second half winners. It was the 34th time the Yankees participated in post-season action while it marked the first appearance in playoff competition for the Brewers. New York took the best of five series, three-games-to-two, for the East pennant. The Yankees went on to sweep the Oakland A's, four-games-to-none, for the American League championship. New York then took on the National League Champion, Los Angeles Dodgers and lost four-games-to-two in the 78th World Series.

Game 1   Yankees 5 – Brewers 3   October 7

New York	ab	r	h	rbi	Milwaukee	ab	r	h	rbi
Randolph 2b	5	0	0	0	Molitor rf	4	0	0	0
Mumphrey cf	5	1	2	0	Yount ss	2	1	1	1
Winfield lf	5	0	1	0	Cooper 1b	3	0	1	0
Jackson rf	4	1	1	0	Simmons c	4	0	1	1
Nettles 3b	5	0	0	0	Thomas cf	4	0	0	0
Gamble dh	4	1	3	2	Ogilvie lf	4	0	0	0
Watson 1b	4	1	3	0	Bando 3b	4	1	1	0
Milbourne ss	4	1	1	0	Moore dh	2	0	2	1
Cerone c	4	0	2	2	Howell dh	2	0	1	0
					Gantner 2b	4	1	1	0
Totals	40	5	13	4	Totals	33	2	8	3

```
New York  ...... 000 400 001 — 5
Milwaukee ..... 011 010 000 — 3
```

E – Gantner, Cerone, Simmons, Yount. DP – Milwaukee 1. LOB – New York 9, Milwaukee 7. 2B – Bando, Gantner, Cerone 2, Gamble. HR – Gamble (1). SB – Yount, Mumphrey. S – Molitor. SF – Yount.

New York	IP	H	R	ER	BB	SO
Guidry	4.1	7	3	3	2	5
RDavis (W 1–0)	2.2	0	0	0	0	0
Gossage (S 1)	2.0	1	0	0	0	3
Milwaukee						
Haas (L 0–1)	3.1	8	4	4	1	1
Bernard	0.2	0	0	0	0	0
McClure	1.1	3	0	0	0	0
Slaton	1.1	1	1	0	0	1
Fingers	1.1	1	1	0	0	1

T – 2:57. A – 35,064.

Game 2   Yankees 3 – Brewers 0   October 8

New York	ab	r	h	rbi	Milwaukee	ab	r	h	rbi
Randolph 2b	4	0	2	0	Molitor rf	4	0	1	0
Mumphrey cf	4	0	0	0	Yount ss	5	0	0	0
Winfield lf	4	1	3	0	Cooper 1b	4	0	1	0
Jackson rf	4	1	1	2	Simmons c	3	0	1	0
Piniella dh	4	1	1	1	Thomas cf	4	0	0	0
Nettles 3b	4	0	0	0	Ogilvie lf	4	0	0	0
Watson 1b	3	0	0	0	Bando 3b	4	0	3	0
Milbourne ss	3	0	0	0	Moore dh	2	0	0	0
Cerone c	3	0	0	0	Howell dh	0	0	0	0
					Bosley dh	0	0	0	0
					Money dh	1	0	0	0
					Gantner 2b	4	0	1	0
Totals	33	3	7	3	Totals	34	0	7	0

```
New York  ...... 000 100 002 – 3
Milwaukee ..... 000 000 000 – 0
```

DP – Milwaukee 1. LOB – New York 3, Milwaukee 11. 2B – Bando, Winfield. HR – Piniella (1), Jackson (1).

New York	IP	H	R	ER	BB	SO
Righetti (W 1–0)	6.0	4	0	0	2	10
RDavis	0.1	1	0	0	2	0
Gossage (S 2)	2.2	2	0	0	0	4
Milwaukee						
Caldwell (L 0–1)	8.1	7	3	3	0	4
Slaton	0.2	0	0	0	0	0

WP – Davis. T – 2:30. A – 26,395

Game 3   Brewers 5 – Yankees 3   October 9

Milwaukee	ab	r	h	rbi	New York	ab	r	h	rbi
Molitor cf	4	1	3	1	Randolph 2b	5	0	1	1
Yount ss	4	1	1	0	Mumphrey cf	4	0	0	0
Cooper 1b	4	1	1	0	Winfield lf	3	1	2	2
Simmons c	3	1	2	3	Jackson rf	4	0	0	0
Thomas dh	4	1	1	0	Piniella dh	3	0	0	0
Ogilvie lf	3	0	0	0	Gamble dh	1	0	1	0
Bando 3b	4	0	1	1	Nettles 3b	2	0	0	0
Moore rf	2	0	0	0	Murcer ph	1	0	0	0
Edwards rf	1	0	0	0	Revering 1b	0	0	0	0
Gantner 2b	3	0	0	0	Milbourne ss	4	1	1	0
					Cerone c	4	0	1	1
Totals	32	5	9	5	Totals	33	3	8	3

```
Milwaukee ..... 000 000 320 – 5
New York  ...... 000 100 200 – 3
```

E – Watson, RMay. DP – Milwaukee 1, New York 1. LOB – Milwaukee 3, New York 7. 2B – Winfield, Simmons. HR – Simmons (1). S – Ogilvie.

Milwaukee	IP	H	R	ER	BB	SO
Lerch	6.0	3	1	1	4	3
Fingers (W 1–0)	3.0	5	2	2	0	3
New York						
John	7.0	8	5	5	2	0
May	2.0	1	0	0	0	1

John pitched to two batters in the 8th. WP – RMay. T – 2:39. A – 56,411.

Game 4   Brewers 2 – Yankees 1   October 10

Milwaukee	ab	r	h	rbi	New York	ab	r	h	rbi
Molitor cf	4	1	1	0	Randolph 2b	3	0	0	0
Yount ss	3	1	1	0	Mumphrey cf	4	1	0	0
Cooper 1b	3	0	0	1	Winfield lf	4	0	1	0
Simmons c	4	0	0	0	Jackson rf	4	0	1	0
Ogilvie lf	3	0	1	1	Gamble dh	1	0	0	0
Thomas cf	3	0	0	0	Piniella dh	2	0	0	1
Edwards cf	0	0	0	0	Nettles 3b	3	0	0	0
Howell dh	3	0	1	0	Watson 1b	3	0	1	0
Bando 3b	3	0	0	0	Brown pr	0	0	0	0
Gantner 2b	3	0	0	0	Revering 1b	0	0	0	0
					Foote ph	0	0	0	0
					Murcer ph	0	0	0	0
					Milbourne ss	4	0	1	0
					Cerone c	4	0	1	0
Totals	29	2	4	2	Totals	32	1	5	1

```
Milwaukee ..... 000 200 000 – 2
New York  ...... 000 001 200 – 1
```

E – Cooper, Gantner. LOB – Milwaukee 2, New York 8. 2B – Ogilvie, Winfield. SF – Cooper.

Milwaukee	IP	H	R	ER	BB	SO
Vuckovich (W 1–0)	5.0	2	1	0	3	4
Easterly	1.0	0	0	0	0	1
Slaton	1.2	2	0	0	0	1
McClure	1.0	0	0	0	0	1
Fingers (S 1)	0.1	1	0	0	1	1
New York						
Reuschel (L 0–1)	6.0	4	2	2	1	3
Davis	3.0	0	0	0	0	2

Vuckovich pitched to two batters in 6th. WP – Vuckovich. T – 2:34. A – 52,077.

Game 5   Yankees 7 – Brewers 3   October 11

Milwaukee	ab	r	h	rbi	New York	ab	r	h	rbi
Molitor cf	4	0	0	0	Mumphrey cf	4	0	0	0
Yount ss	5	1	3	0	Milbourne ss	4	2	3	0
Cooper 1b	4	0	1	2	Winfield lf	4	0	0	0
Simmons c	4	0	0	0	Jackson rf	4	2	3	2
Thomas dh	4	1	1	1	Gamble dh	3	1	1	1
Ogilvie lf	4	0	2	0	Piniella dh	1	0	1	0
Bando 3b	2	0	0	0	Nettles 3b	3	1	1	1
Moore rf	3	0	0	0	Watson 1b	4	0	1	0
Howell ph	0	0	0	0	Cerone c	3	1	2	2
Edwards rf	0	0	0	0	Randolph 2b	3	0	1	0
Romero 2b	2	1	1	0					
Money 2b	2	0	0	0					
Totals	34	3	8	3	Totals	33	7	13	7

```
Milwaukee ..... 011 000 100 – 3
New York  ...... 000 400 12X – 7
```

DP – Milwaukee 3. LOB – Milwaukee 9, New York 3. 2B – Milbourne, Piniella. 3B – Yount. HR – Thomas (1), Jackson (2), Gamble (2), Cerone (1). SF – Cooper, Nettles.

Milwaukee	IP	H	R	ER	BB	SO
Haas (W 0–2)	3.1	5	3	3	0	0
Caldwell	0.0	2	1	1	0	0
Bernard	1.2	0	0	0	0	0
McClure	1.0	1	0	0	0	1
Slaton	1.1	3	2	2	0	0
Easterly	0.1	2	1	1	0	0
Vuckovich	0.1	0	0	0	0	0
New York						
Guidry	4.0	4	2	2	1	3
Righetti (W 2–0)	3.0	4	1	1	1	3
Gossage	2.0	0	0	0	2	1

Caldwell pitched to two batters in 4th.
T – 2:47. A – 47,505.

1982 AMERICAN LEAGUE CHAMPIONSHIP SERIES

MILWAUKEE BREWERS vs CALIFORNIA ANGELS

In a dramatic and thrilling ALCS, Milwaukee sets a precedent in post-season play by rallying from a two-games-to-none deficit and earn its first American League pennant in defeating California, three-games-to-two. The Angels captured the first two games — both played in Anaheim Stadium. The Brewers comeback occurred at home where they won three straight games at County Stadium, the first time a club accomplished the feat.

Game 1   Angels 8 – Brewers 3   October 5

Milwaukee	ab	r	h	rbi	California	ab	r	h	rbi
Molitor 3b	4	1	1	0	Downing lf	4	2	1	0
Yount ss	4	0	1	0	Beniquez lf	0	0	0	0
Cooper 1b	4	0	1	1	DeCinces 3b	4	2	1	0
Simmons c	4	1	2	0	Grich 2b	3	1	2	1
Thomas cf	4	1	1	2	Baylor dh	3	1	2	5
Oglivie lf	4	0	0	0	ReJackson rf	4	0	0	1
Money dh	3	0	0	0	Clark rf	0	0	0	0
Moore rf	3	0	1	0	Lynn cf	4	1	3	1
Gantner 2b	4	0	0	0	Carew 1b	4	0	0	0
					Foli ss	4	0	0	0
					Boone c	4	1	1	0
Totals	34	3	7	3	Totals	34	8	10	8

```
Milwaukee  . . . . . 021 000 000 – 3
California . . . . . . 104 210 00X – 8
```

E – Caldwell, Molitor. DP – Milwaukee 1. LOB – Milwaukee 6, California 5. 2B – Cooper, Grich. 3B – Baylor. HR – Thomas (1), Lynn (1) SF – Baylor.

Milwaukee	IP	H	R	ER	BB	SO
Caldwell (L 0–1)	3.0	7	6	5	1	2
Slaton	3.0	3	2	1	1	2
Ladd	1.0	0	0	0	0	3
Bernard	1.0	0	0	0	0	0
California						
John (W 1–0)	9.0	7	3	3	1	5

Caldwell pitched to one batter in 4th. Game Winning RBI – Baylor. HBP – By John (Moore). WP – Caldwell. T – 2:31. A – 64,406.

Game 2   Angels 4 – Brewers 2   October 6

Milwaukee	ab	r	h	rbi	California	ab	r	h	rbi
Molitor 3b	4	1	2	2	Downing lf	3	0	0	0
Yount ss	4	0	1	0	Beniquez lf	0	0	0	0
Cooper 1b	4	0	0	0	Carew 1b	4	0	0	0
Simmons c	4	0	0	0	ReJackson rf	3	1	1	1
Oglivie lf	4	0	0	0	Clark rf	0	0	0	0
Thomas cf	3	0	0	0	Lynn cf	4	1	2	0
Howell dh	3	0	0	0	Baylor dh	3	0	0	0
Moore rf	3	1	2	0	DeCinces 3b	3	2	1	0
Gantner 2b	3	0	0	0	Grich 2b	2	0	1	0
					Foli ss	2	0	1	1
					Boone c	1	0	0	2
Totals	32	2	5	2	Totals	25	4	6	4

```
Milwaukee  . . . . . 000 020 000 – 2
California . . . . . . 021 100 00X – 4
```

E – None. DP – Milwaukee 2. LOB – Milwaukee 3, California 5. 2B – DeCinces. HR – ReJackson (1), Molitor (1). SH – Boone, Foli. SF – Boone.

Milwaukee	IP	H	R	ER	BB	SO
Vuckovich (L 0–1)	8.0	6	4	4	4	4
California						
Kison (W 1–0)	9.0	5	2	2	0	8

Game Winning RBI – Foli. HBP – By Vuckovich (Grich). T – 2:06. A – 64,179.

Game 3   Brewers 5 – Angels 3   October 8

California	ab	r	h	rbi	Milwaukee	ab	r	h	rbi
Downing lf	4	0	0	0	Molitor 3b	4	1	1	2
Carew 1b	4	1	2	0	Yount ss	2	1	1	0
ReJackson rf	4	0	1	0	Cooper 1b	4	1	1	1
Lynn cf	3	1	2	1	Simmons c	4	1	1	0
Baylor dh	3	0	1	1	Thomas cf	3	0	0	1
DeCinces 3b	4	0	1	0	Oglivie lf	3	0	1	0
Grich 2b	4	0	0	0	Money dh	1	0	0	1
Foli ss	3	0	0	0	Edwards pr-dh	0	1	0	0
Wilfong ph	1	0	0	0	Moore rf	2	0	1	0
Boone c	4	1	1	1	Gantner 2b	3	0	0	0
Totals	34	3	8	3	Totals	26	5	6	5

```
California . . . . . . 000 000 030 – 3
Milwaukee  . . . . . 000 300 20X – 5
```

E – None. DP – California 1, Milwaukee 1. LOB – California 6, Milwaukee 4. 2B – Lynn, Baylor, Cooper. HR – Molitor (2), Boone (1). SB – Carew. SH – Moore. SF – Thomas, Money.

California	IP	H	R	ER	BB	SO
Zahn (L 0–1)	3.2	4	3	3	1	2
Witt	3.0	2	2	2	2	3
Hassler	1.1	0	0	0	0	1
Milwaukee						
Sutton (W 1–0)	7.2	8	3	3	2	9
Ladd (S 1)	1.1	0	0	0	0	2

Game Winning RBI – Cooper. HBP – By Zahn (Oglivie). T – 2:41. A – 50,135.

Game 4   Brewers 9 – Angels 5   October 9

California	ab	r	h	rbi	Milwaukee	ab	r	h	rbi
Downing lf	4	1	1	0	Molitor 3b	4	0	0	1
Carew 1b	2	1	0	0	Yount ss	4	0	1	0
ReJackson rf	4	1	0	0	Cooper 1b	4	0	0	0
Lynn cf	3	1	1	1	Simmons c	3	1	0	0
Baylor dh	4	1	1	4	Thomas cf	2	0	0	0
DeCinces 3b	4	0	1	0	Money dh	3	2	2	0
Grich 2b	3	0	0	0	Edwards pr-dh	0	1	0	0
Foli ss	4	0	1	0	Brouhard lf	4	4	3	3
Boone c	4	0	0	0	Moore rf	2	1	1	0
					Gantner 2b	4	0	2	2
Totals	32	5	5	5	Totals	30	9	9	6

```
California . . . . . . 000 001 040 – 5
Milwaukee  . . . . . 030 301 02X – 9
```

E – Lynn, DeCinces 2, Yount, Cooper. DP – California 1. LOB – California 5, Milwaukee 5. 2B – Lynn, Carew, Brouhard. HR – Baylor (1), Brouhard (1). SB – Edwards. CS – Carew, Molitor, Thomas. SH – Moore.

California	IP	H	R	ER	BB	SO
John (L 1–1)	3.1	4	6	4	5	1
Goltz	3.2	4	3	3	2	2
Sanchez	1.0	1	0	0	0	0
Milwaukee						
Haas (W 1–0)	7.1	5	5	4	5	7
Slaton (S 1)	1.2	0	0	0	0	1

Goltz pitched to two batters in 8th. Game Winning RBI – Brouhard. WP – John 3. PB – Boone. T – 3:10. A – 51,003.

Game 5   Brewers 4 – Angels 3   October 10

California	ab	r	h	rbi	Milwaukee	ab	r	h	rbi
Downing lf	4	1	1	0	Molitor 3b	3	1	2	0
Carew 1b	3	0	0	0	Yount ss	2	0	0	0
ReJackson rf	3	0	0	0	Cooper 1b	4	0	1	2
Lynn cf	4	0	3	2	Simmons c	3	0	0	1
Baylor dh	4	0	1	0	Oglivie lf	4	1	1	1
DeCinces 3b	4	1	3	0	Thomas cf	3	0	0	0
Grich 2b	3	0	0	0	Edwards cf	1	0	0	0
Foli ss	3	0	0	0	Money dh	4	0	0	0
RoJackson ph	1	0	1	0	Moore rf	3	1	1	0
Wilfong pr	0	0	0	0	Gantner 2b	2	1	1	0
Boone c	3	1	2	1					
Totals	32	3	11	3	Totals	29	4	6	4

```
California . . . . . . 101 100 000 – 3
Milwaukee  . . . . . 100 100 20X – 4
```

E – Oglivie 2, Molitor, Cooper, DeCinces. DP – California 1, Milwaukee 2. LOB – California 8, Milwaukee 6. 2B – Downing, DeCinces, Molitor. HR – Oglivie (1). SB – Molitor. CS – DeCinces. SH – Downing, Grich, Boone. SF – Simmons.

California	IP	H	R	ER	BB	SO
Kison	5.0	3	2	1	3	4
Sanchez (L 0–1)	1.2	3	2	2	1	1
Hassler	1.1	0	0	0	0	1
Milwaukee						
Vuckovich	6.1	9	3	3	3	4
McClure (W 1–0)	1.2	2	0	0	0	0
Ladd (S 2)	1.0	0	0	0	0	0

McClure pitched to one batter in 9th. Game Winning RBI – Cooper. T – 3:01. A – 54,968.

1982 79TH WORLD SERIES

MILWAUKEE BREWERS
vs
ST. LOUIS CARDINALS

It was labeled the "Suds Series," and the 79th World Series between Milwaukee and St. Louis truly foamed over with exciting action as it went the full seven-game limit. The Series is tied three times and each club held the advantage twice in the see-saw battle. The Cardinals, making their 13th visit to the Fall Classic, won for the ninth time, taking the Brewers, who were making their first trip, four-games-to-three.

Game 1 Brewers 10 – Cardinals 0 October 12

Milwaukee	ab	r	h	rbi	St. Louis	ab	r	h	rbi
Molitor 3b	6	1	5	2	Herr 2b	3	0	0	0
Yount ss	6	1	4	2	LSmith lf	4	0	0	0
Cooper 1b	4	1	0	0	Hernandez 1b	4	0	0	0
Simmons c	5	1	2	1	Hendrick rf	4	0	0	0
Oglivie lf	4	1	0	0	Tenace dh	3	0	0	0
Thomas cf	4	0	1	1	Porter c	3	0	2	0
Howell dh	2	0	0	0	Green cf	3	0	0	0
Money dh	2	1	1	1	Oberkfell 3b	3	0	1	0
Moore rf	5	2	2	0	OSmith ss	3	0	0	0
Gantner 2b	4	2	2	2					
Totals	42	10	17	9	Totals	30	0	3	0

Milwaukee ..... 200 112 004 – 10
St. Louis ...... 000 000 000 – 0

E – Hernandez. DP – St. Louis 1. LOB – Milwaukee 10, St. Louis 4. 2B – Porter, Moore, Yount. 3B – Gantner. HR – Simmons (1). S – Gantner.

Milwaukee	IP	H	R	ER	BB	SO
Caldwell (W 1–0)	9.0	3	0	0	1	3
St. Louis						
Forsch (L 0–1)	5.2	10	6	4	1	1
Kaat	1.1	1	0	0	1	1
LaPoint	1.2	3	2	2	1	0
Lahti	0.1	3	2	2	0	1

HBP – by Forsch (Howell). T – 2:30. A – 53,723.

Game 2 Cardinals 5 – Brewers 4 October 13

Milwaukee	ab	r	h	rbi	St. Louis	ab	r	h	rbi
Molitor 3b	5	1	2	0	Herr 2b	3	1	1	1
Yount ss	4	1	1	1	Oberkfell 3b	3	1	2	1
Cooper 1b	5	0	3	2	Tenace ph	1	0	0	0
Simmons c	3	1	1	1	Ramsey 3b	0	0	0	0
Oglivie lf	4	0	1	0	Hernandez 1b	3	0	0	0
Thomas cf	3	0	0	0	Porter c	4	0	2	2
Howell dh	4	1	0	0	LSmith lf	3	0	0	0
Moore rf	4	0	2	1	Iorg dh	2	0	1	0
Gantner 2b	3	0	0	0	Green ph	1	0	0	0
					Braun ph	0	0	0	1
					McGee cf	4	1	0	0
					OSmith ss	4	0	2	0
Totals	35	4	10	4	Totals	31	5	8	5

Milwaukee ..... 012 010 000 – 4
St. Louis ...... 002 002 01X – 5

E – Oglivie. DP – St. Louis 1. LOB – Milwaukee 8, St. Louis 7. 2B – Moore, Herr, Yount, Porter, Cooper. HR – Simmons (2). SB – Molitor (1), McGee (1), Oberkfell (1), OSmith (1).

Milwaukee	IP	H	R	ER	BB	SO
Sutton	6.0	5	4	4	1	3
McClure (L 0–1)	1.1	2	1	1	2	2
Ladd	0.2	1	0	0	2	0
St. Louis						
Stuper	4.0	6	4	4	3	3
Kaat	0.2	1	0	0	0	0
Bair	2.0	1	0	0	0	3
Sutter (W 1–0)	2.1	2	0	0	1	1

Stuper pitched to one batter in 5th.
WP – Stuper 2. T – 2:54. A – 53,723.

Game 3 Cardinals 6 – Brewers 2 October 15

St. Louis	ab	r	h	rbi	Milwaukee	ab	r	h	rbi
Herr 2b	5	0	0	0	Molitor 3b	4	0	0	0
Oberkfell 3b	4	0	0	0	Yount ss	3	1	0	0
Hernandez 1b	4	0	0	0	Cooper 1b	4	1	1	2
Hendrick rf	2	1	1	0	Simmons c	4	0	1	0
Porter c	4	0	0	0					
					Oglivie lf	4	0	0	0
LSmith lf	4	2	2	0	Thomas cf	4	0	1	0
Green lf	0	0	0	0	Howell dh	2	0	0	0
Iorg dh	4	1	1	0	a – Money dh	1	0	0	0
McGee cf	3	2	2	4	Moore rf	3	0	0	0
OSmith ss	3	0	0	1	Gantner 2b	3	0	2	0
Totals	33	6	6	5	Totals	32	2	5	2

a – Money walked for Howell in 7th.

St. Louis ...... 000 030 231 – 6
Milwaukee ..... 000 000 020 – 2

Hendrick reached base on catcher's interference in 9th. E – Cooper, Gantner, Simmons, Hernandez. DP – St. Louis 1. LOB – St. Louis 4, Milwaukee 6. 2B – Gantner, LSmith, Iorg. 3B – LSmith. HR – McGee 2(2), Cooper (1).

St. Louis	IP	H	R	ER	BB	SO
Andujar (W 1–0)	6.1	3	0	0	1	3
Kaat	0.1	1	0	0	1	0
Bair	0.0	0	0	0	0	0
Sutter (S 1)	2.1	1	2	2	1	1
Milwaukee						
Vuckovich (L 0–1)	8.2	6	6	4	3	1
McClure	0.1	0	0	0	0	0

Bair pitched to one batter in 7th.
T – 2:53. A – 56,556.

Game 4 Brewers 7 – Cardinals 5 October 16

St. Louis	ab	r	h	rbi	Milwaukee	ab	r	h	rbi
Herr 2b	4	0	0	2	Molitor 3b	4	1	0	0
Oberkfell 3b	2	2	1	0	Yount ss	4	1	2	2
Tenace 1b	1	0	0	0	Cooper 1b	4	1	2	1
Hernandez, 1b	4	0	0	0	Simmons c	2	0	0	0
Hendrick rf	4	0	1	1	Thomas cf	4	0	1	2
Porter c	3	0	1	0	Oglivie lf	3	1	1	0
LSmith lf	4	1	1	0	Money dh	4	2	2	0
Iorg dh	4	0	2	1	Moore rf	4	0	1	0
Green pr	0	0	0	0	Gantner 2b	4	1	1	1
McGee cf	4	1	1	0					
OSmith ss	3	1	1	0					
Totals	33	5	8	4	Totals	33	7	10	6

St. Louis ...... 130 001 000 – 5
Milwaukee ..... 000 010 60X – 7

E – Gantner, Yount, LaPoint. DP – St. Louis 2, Milwaukee 2. LOB – St. Louis 6, Milwaukee 6. 2B – Oberkfell, Money, LSmith, Iorg, Gantner. 3B – Oglivie. SB – McGee, Oberkfell. SF – Herr.

St. Louis	IP	H	R	ER	BB	SO
LaPoint	6.2	7	4	1	1	3
Bair (L 0–1)	0.0	1	2	2	1	0
Kaat	0.0	1	1	1	1	0
Lahti	1.1	1	0	0	1	0
Milwaukee						
Haas	5.1	7	5	4	2	3
Slaton (W 1–0)	2.0	1	0	0	2	1
McClure (S 1)	1.2	0	0	0	0	2

Bair pitched to two batters in 7th.
Kaat pitched to two batters in 7th.
WP – Haas, Kaat. T – 3:04. A – 56,560.

Game 5 Brewers 6 – Cardinals 4 October 17

St. Louis	ab	r	h	rbi	Milwaukee	ab	r	h	rbi
LSmith dh	5	0	2	0	Molitor 3b	4	1	1	1
Green lf	5	2	2	0	Yount ss	4	2	4	1
Hernandez 1b	4	1	3	2	Cooper 1b	4	0	1	1
Hendrick rf	5	0	3	2	Simmons c	3	0	0	1
Porter c	5	0	1	0	Oglivie lf	4	1	2	0
Ramsey pr	0	0	0	0	Thomas cf	4	0	0	0
McGee cf	5	0	1	0	Money dh	3	1	0	0
Oberkfell 3b	4	0	3	0	Moore rf	4	1	2	1
Tenace ph	1	0	0	0	Gantner 2b	4	0	1	1
Herr 2b	4	0	0	0					
OSmith ss	3	1	0	0					
Totals	41	4	15	4	Totals	34	6	11	6

St. Louis ...... 001 000 102 – 4
Milwaukee ..... 101 010 12x – 6

E – Forsch, Gantner, Herr. DP – St. Louis 2, Milwaukee 2. LOB – St. Louis 12, Milwaukee 7. 2B – Hernandez 2, Yount, Moore, Green. 3B – Green. SB – Yount (1). SB – LSmith.

St. Louis	IP	H	R	ER	BB	SO
Forsch (L 0–2)	7.0	8	4	3	2	3
Sutter	1.0	3	2	2	1	2
Milwaukee						
Caldwell (W 2–0)	8.1	14	4	4	2	3
McClure (S 2)	0.2	1	0	0	0	1

T – 3:02. A – 56,562.

BREWERS POST SEASON

Game 6   Cardinals 13 – Brewers 1   October 19

Milwaukee	ab	r	h	rbi	St. Louis	ab	r	h	rbi
Molitor 3b	4	0	1	0	LSmith lf	3	1	1	0
Yount ss	4	0	0	0	Green lf	1	1	0	0
Cooper 1b	4	0	0	0	Oberkfell 3b	5	1	0	0
Simmons c	2	0	0	0	Hernandez 1b	5	2	2	4
Yost c	0	0	0	0	Hendrick rf	5	2	2	1
Oglivie lf	4	0	1	0	Porter c	4	1	1	2
Thomas cf	3	0	0	0	Brummer c	0	0	0	0
Edwards cf	0	0	0	0	Iorg dh	4	3	3	0
Money dh	3	0	0	0	McGee cf	4	1	1	1
Moore rf	3	0	1	0	Herr 2b	3	1	2	2
Gantner 2b	3	1	1	0	OSmith ss	4	0	0	0
Totals	30	1	4	0	Totals	38	13	12	10

```
Milwaukee  . . . . . 000 000 001 – 1
St. Louis  . . . . . . . 020 326 00X – 13
```

E – Yount 2, Gantner 2, Oberkfell. DP – St. Louis 2. LOB – Milwaukee 4, St. Louis 3.
2B – Iorg 2, Herr, Gantner. 3B – Iorg. HR – Porter (1), Hernandez (1). SB – LSmith. S – Herr.

Milwaukee	IP	H	R	ER	BB	SO
Sutton (L 0–1)	4.1	7	7	5	0	2
Slaton	0.2	0	0	0	0	0
Medich	2.0	5	6	4	1	0
Bernard	1.0	0	0	0	0	1
St. Louis						
Super (W 1–0)	9.0	4	1	1	2	2

WP – Medich 2, Stuper. Balk – Sutton. T – 2:21. A – 53,723.

Game 7   Cardinals 6 – Brewers 3   October 20

Milwaukee	ab	r	h	rbi	St. Louis	ab	r	h	rbi
Molitor 3b	4	1	2	0	LSmith lf	5	2	3	1
Yount ss	4	0	1	0	Oberkfell 3b	3	0	0	0
Cooper 1b	3	0	1	1	Tenace ph	0	0	0	0
Simmons c	4	0	0	0	Ramsey 3b	1	1	0	0
Oglivie lf	4	1	1	1	Hernandez 1b	3	1	2	2
Thomas cf	4	0	0	0	Hendrick rf	5	0	2	1
Howell dh	3	0	0	0	Porter c	5	0	1	1
Moore rf	3	0	1	0	Iorg dh	3	0	2	0
Gantner 2b	3	1	1	0	Green ph	0	0	0	0
					Braun dh	2	0	1	1
					McGee cf	5	1	1	0
					Herr 2b	3	0	1	0
Totals	32	3	7	2	OSmith ss	4	1	2	0
					Totals	39	6	15	6

```
Milwaukee  . . . . . 000 012 000 – 3
St. Louis  . . . . . . . 000 103 02X – 6
```

E – Andujar. LOB – Milwaukee 3, St. Louis 13. 2B – Gantner, LSmith 2. HR – Oglivie (1).
SF – Cooper.

Milwaukee	IP	H	R	ER	BB	SO
Vuckovich	5.1	10	3	3	2	3
McClure (L 0–2)	0.1	2	1	1	1	0
Haas	2.0	1	2	2	1	1
Caldwell	0.1	2	0	0	0	0
St. Louis						
Andujar (W 2–0)	7.0	7	3	2	0	1
Sutter (S 2)	2.0	0	0	0	0	2

T – 2:50. A – 53,723.

Down Through History at County Stadium

ROBIN YOUNT, September 9, 1992 — Becomes the 17th player and 3rd youngest in major league history to collect 3,000 career hits, singling in the 7th inning off Cleveland's Jose Mesa.

ROBIN YOUNT, September 24, 1991 — With a 3rd inning single off New York's Eric Plunk, he becomes only the 37th player (13th in the American League) to collect 2,000 career singles.

PAUL MOLITOR, September 23, 1991 — Matches the club single season record with his 6th lead off home run of the year (shared by Tommy Harper, 1970).

CECIL FIELDER, September 14, 1991 — Hits a 502 foot home run that clears the left field bleachers. It is the longest County Stadium home run in the history of the Milwaukee Brewers.

JIM GANTNER, September 3, 1991 — Hits his first home run in 544 games (1,762 at bats). It ends the longest active homerless streak in the majors. Gantner hits his homer off Oakland's Dave Stewart in the 7th inning.

PAUL MOLITOR, July 30, 1991 — Collected his 2,000th career hit off Kansas City's Bret Saberhagen.

WILLIE RANDOLPH, April 15, 1991 — Collected his 2,000th career hit off Baltimore's Mark Williamson.

MILWAUKEE BREWERS, July 8, 1990 — Trailing 7–0, the Brewers stage a comeback to win 20–7. Milwaukee scores a club record 13 runs in the 5th inning. Eighteen batters come to the plate in the record frame.

NOLAN RYAN, July 31, 1990 — Wins his 300th career game.

JOSE CANSECO, September 23, 1988 — Steals his 40th base of the year, making him the first player to ever steal 40 bases and hit 40 home runs in the same season.

PAUL MOLITOR, August 25, 1987 — Hits safely in 39 straight games, the 5th longest hitting streak in modern day history.

MILWAUKEE BREWERS, April 19, 1987 — Set an American League record by opening the campaign with 12 straight victories. The following night in Chicago, the club ties the major league mark with a 13–0 start.

DON SUTTON, June 24, 1983 — Becomes only the 8th pitcher to collect 3,000 career strikeouts.

MILWAUKEE BREWERS, October 10, 1982 — Capture their lone American League pennant, becoming the first club ever to rally from a 0–2 deficit to win a pennant.

RICKEY HENDERSON, August 27, 1982 — Steals his 119th base (surpassing Lou Brock's mark) enroute to a major league record 130 steals in a single season.

STEVE BUSBY, June 19, 1974 — With Kansas City, pitches the only no-hitter ever against the Brewers.

TOMMY HARPER, September 22, 1970 — Hits his 30th home run (finished with 31) and coupled with 32 stolen bases (finished with 38) becomes only the 5th player to join the elite 30/30 club.